INDIAN COOKBOOK 2022

AUTHENTIC REGIONAL RECIPES

MEL GREENE

Table of Contents

Murgh Bagan-e-Bahar 18
    Ingredients 18
    Method 19
Butter Chicken 20
    Ingredients 20
    Method 21
Chicken Sukha 22
    Ingredients 22
    Method 23
Indian Roast Chicken 24
    Ingredients 24
    Method 25
Spicy Scramble 26
    Ingredients 26
    Method 26
Chicken Curry with Dry Coconut 27
    Ingredients 27
    Method 28
Simple Chicken 29
    Ingredients 29
    Method 30
Southern Chicken Curry 31
    Ingredients 31

For the seasoning: 32
    Method 32
Chicken Stew in Coconut Milk 33
    Ingredients 33
    Method 34
Chandi Tikka 35
    Ingredients 35
    Method 36
Tandoori Chicken 37
    Ingredients 37
    Method 38
Murgh Lajawab 39
    Ingredients 39
    Method 40
Lahori Chicken 41
    Ingredients 41
    Method 42
Chicken Liver 43
    Ingredients 43
    Method 43
Balti Chicken 44
    Ingredients 44
    Method 45
Tangy Chicken 46
    Ingredients 46
    Method 47
Chicken Dilruba 48

- Ingredients 48
  - Method 49
- Fried Chicken Wings 50
  - Ingredients 50
  - Method 50
- Murgh Mussalam 51
  - Ingredients 51
  - Method 52
- Chicken Delight 53
  - Ingredients 53
  - Method 54
- Salli Chicken 55
  - Ingredients 55
  - Method 56
- Fried Chicken Tikka 57
  - Ingredients 57
  - Method 58
- Chicken Seekh 59
  - Ingredients 59
  - Method 59
- Nadan Kozhikari 60
  - Ingredients 60
  - Method 61
- Mum's Chicken 62
  - Ingredients 62
  - Method 63
- Methi Chicken 64

- Ingredients 64
- Method 65
- Spicy Chicken Drumsticks 66
  - Ingredients 66
  - For the spice mixture: 66
  - Method 67
- Dieter's Chicken Curry 68
  - Ingredients 68
  - Method 69
- Heavenly Chicken 70
  - Ingredients 70
  - For the spice mixture: 70
  - Method 71
- Chicken Rizala 72
  - Ingredients 72
  - Method 73
- Chicken Surprise 74
  - Ingredients 74
  - Method 75
- Cheesy Chicken 76
  - Ingredients 76
  - For the marinade: 76
  - Method 77
- Beef Korma 78
  - Ingredients 78
  - For the spice mixture: 78
  - Method 79

Dhal Kheema 80
    Ingredients 80
    For the spice mixture: 80
    Method 81
Pork Curry 82
    Ingredients 82
    For the spice mixture: 82
    Method 83
Shikampoore Kebab 84
    Ingredients 84
    Method 85
Special Mutton 87
    Ingredients 87
    For the spice mixture: 87
    Method 88
Green Masala Chops 89
    Ingredients 89
    For the spice mixture: 89
    Method 90
Layered Kebab 91
    Ingredients 91
    For the white layer: 91
    For the green layer: 91
    For the orange layer: 92
    For the meat layer: 92
    Method 92
Barrah Champ 94

- Ingredients 94
  - Method 95
- Lamb Pickle 96
  - Ingredients 96
  - Method 97
- Goan Lamb Curry 98
  - Ingredients 98
  - For the spice mixture: 98
  - Method 99
- Bagara Meat 100
  - Ingredients 100
  - For the spice mixture: 100
  - Method 101
- Liver in Coconut Milk 102
  - Ingredients 102
  - For the spice mixture: 102
  - Method 103
- Lamb Masala with Yoghurt 104
  - Ingredients 104
  - For the spice mixture: 104
  - Method 105
- Korma in Khada Masala 106
  - Ingredients 106
  - Method 107
- Lamb & Kidney Curry 108
  - Ingredients 108
  - For the spice mixture: 109

- Method 109
- Gosht Gulfaam 111
  - Ingredients 111
  - For the sauce: 111
  - Method 112
- Lamb Do Pyaaza 113
  - Ingredients 113
  - Method 114
- Fish Kebab 114
  - Ingredients 115
  - For the stuffing: 115
  - Method 116
- Fish Chops 118
  - Ingredients 118
  - Method 119
- Fish Sookha 121
  - Ingredients 121
  - Method 122
- Mahya Kalia 123
  - Ingredients 123
  - Method 124
- Prawn Curry Rosachi 125
  - Ingredients 125
  - Method 126
- Fish Stuffed with Dates & Almonds 127
  - Ingredients 127
  - Method 127

Tandoori Fish 129
    Ingredients 129
    Method 129
Fish with Vegetables 130
    Ingredients 130
    Method 131
Tandoor Gulnar 132
    Ingredients 132
    For the first marinade: 132
    For the second marinade: 132
Prawns in Green Masala 133
    Ingredients 133
    Method 134
Fish Cutlet 135
    Ingredients 135
    Method 136
Parsi Fish Sas 137
    Ingredients 137
    Method 138
Peshawari Machhi 139
    Ingredients 139
    Method 139
Crab Curry 140
    Ingredients 140
    Method 141
Mustard Fish 142
    Ingredients 142

    Method 142
Meen Vattichathu 143
    Ingredients 143
    Method 144
Doi Maach 145
    Ingredients 145
    For the marinade: 145
    Method 146
Fish Fry 147
    Ingredients 147
    Method 147
Machher Chop 148
    Ingredients 148
    Method 148
Goa Swordfish 150
    Ingredients 150
    Method 151
Dry Fish Masala 152
    Ingredients 152
    Method 152
Madras Prawn Curry 153
    Ingredients 153
    Method 153
Fish in Fenugreek 154
    Ingredients 154
    Method 155
Karimeen Porichathu 156

- Ingredients 156
- Method 157
- Jumbo Prawns 158
  - Ingredients 158
  - Method 159
- Pickled Fish 160
  - Ingredients 160
  - Method 160
- Fish Ball Curry 161
  - Ingredients 161
  - Method 162
- Fish Amritsari 163
  - Ingredients 163
  - Method 163
- Masala Fried Prawns 164
  - Ingredients 164
  - Method 165
- Savoury Topped Fish 166
  - Ingredients 166
  - Method 167
- Prawn Pasanda 168
  - Ingredients 168
  - Method 169
- Swordfish Rechaido 170
  - Ingredients 170
  - Method 171
- Teekha Jhinga 172

- Ingredients 172
- Method 173
- Prawns Balchow 174
  - Ingredients 174
  - Method 174
- Prawns Bhujna 176
  - Ingredients 176
  - Method 177
- Chingdi Macher Malai 178
  - Ingredients 178
  - Method 179
- Fish Sorse Bata 180
  - Ingredients 180
  - Method 180
- Fish Stew 181
  - Ingredients 181
  - Method 182
- Jhinga Nissa 183
  - Ingredients 183
  - Method 184
- Squid Vindaloo 185
  - Ingredients 185
  - Method 186
- Lobster Balchow 187
  - Ingredients 187
  - Method 188
- Prawns with Aubergine 189

- Ingredients ... 189
  - Method ... 190
- Green Prawns ... 191
  - Ingredients ... 191
  - Method ... 191
- Fish with Coriander ... 192
  - Ingredients ... 192
  - Method ... 192
- Fish Malai ... 193
  - Ingredients ... 193
  - For the spice mixture: ... 193
  - Method ... 194
- Konkani Fish Curry ... 195
  - Ingredients ... 195
  - Method ... 195
- Spicy Prawns with Garlic ... 196
  - Ingredients ... 196
  - Method ... 197
- Simple Fish Curry ... 198
  - Ingredients ... 198
  - Method ... 198
- Goan Fish Curry ... 199
  - Ingredients ... 199
  - Method ... 200
- Prawn Vindaloo ... 201
  - Serves 4 ... 201
  - Ingredients ... 201

Method	202
Fish in Green Masala	203
Ingredients	203
Method	204
Clams Masala	205
Ingredients	205
Method	206
Fish Tikka	207
Ingredients	207
Method	208
Aubergine Stuffed with Prawns	209
Ingredients	209
Method	210
Prawns with Garlic & Cinnamon	211
Ingredients	211
Method	211
Sole Steamed in Mustard	212
Ingredients	212
Method	212
Yellow Fish Curry	213
Ingredients	213
Method	213
Rassa	216
Ingredients	216
Method	216
Doodhi Manpasand	218
Ingredients	218

Method 219

Murgh Bagan-e-Bahar

(Grilled Chicken Drumsticks)

Serves 4

Ingredients

Salt to taste

1½ tsp ginger paste

1½ tsp garlic paste

1 tsp garam masala

8 chicken drumsticks

30g/1oz mint leaves, finely chopped

2 tbsp dried pomegranate seeds

50g/1¾oz yoghurt

1 tsp ground black pepper

Juice of 1 lemon

Chaat masala* to taste

Method

- Mix the salt, ginger paste, garlic paste and garam masala. Make incisions on the drumsticks and marinate them with this mixture for 1 hour.

- Grind together the remaining ingredients, except the chaat masala.

- Mix the ground mixture with the chicken and set aside for 4 hours.

- Grill the chicken for 30 minutes. Sprinkle with the chaat masala. Serve.

Butter Chicken

Serves 4

Ingredients

1kg/2¼lb chicken, chopped into 12 pieces

Salt to taste

1 tsp turmeric

Juice of 1 lemon

4 tbsp butter

3 large onions, finely chopped

1 tsp ginger paste

1 tsp garlic paste

1 tbsp ground coriander

4 large tomatoes, puréed

125g/4½oz yoghurt

Method

- Marinate the chicken with the salt, turmeric and lemon juice for an hour.

- Heat the butter in a saucepan. Add the onions and fry till translucent.

- Add the ginger paste, garlic paste and ground coriander. Fry on a medium heat for 5 minutes.

- Add the marinated chicken. Fry for 5 minutes. Add the tomato purée and yoghurt. Cover with a lid and simmer for 35 minutes. Serve hot.

Chicken Sukha

(Dry Chicken)

Serves 4

Ingredients

2 tbsp refined vegetable oil

4 large onions, finely chopped

1kg/2¼lb chicken, chopped into 12 pieces

4 tomatoes, finely chopped

1 tsp turmeric

2 green chillies, sliced

8 garlic cloves, crushed

5cm/2in root ginger, grated

2 tbsp garam masala

2 cubes chicken stock

Salt to taste

50g/1¾oz coriander leaves, chopped

Method

- Heat the oil in a saucepan. Fry the onions on a medium heat till brown. Add the remaining ingredients, except the coriander leaves.

- Mix well and cook on a low heat for 40 minutes, stirring occasionally.

- Garnish with the coriander leaves. Serve hot.

Indian Roast Chicken

Serves 4

Ingredients

1kg/2¼lb chicken

1 tbsp lemon juice

Salt to taste

2 large onions

2.5cm/1in root ginger

4 garlic cloves

3 cloves

3 green cardamom pods

5cm/2in cinnamon

4 tbsp refined vegetable oil

200g/7oz breadcrumbs

2 apples, chopped

4 hard-boiled eggs, chopped

Method

- Marinate the chicken with the lemon juice and salt for 1 hour.

- Grind together the onions, ginger, garlic, cloves, cardamom and cinnamon with enough water to form a smooth paste.

- Heat the oil in a saucepan. Add the paste and fry on a low heat for 7 minutes. Add the breadcrumbs, apples and salt. Cook for 3-4 minutes.

- Stuff the chicken with this mixture and roast in an oven at 230°C (450°F, Gas Mark 8) for 40 minutes. Garnish with the eggs. Serve hot.

Spicy Scramble

Serves 4

Ingredients

3 tbsp refined vegetable oil

750g/1lb 10oz chicken sausages, sliced

4 green peppers, julienned

1 tsp chilli powder

2 tsp ground cumin

10 garlic cloves, finely chopped

3 tomatoes, quartered

4 tbsp cold water

½ tsp freshly ground pepper

Salt to taste

4 eggs, lightly whisked

Method

- Heat the oil in a saucepan. Add the sausages and fry on a medium heat till brown. Add all the remaining ingredients, except the eggs. Mix well. Cook on a low heat for 8-10 minutes.

- Gently add the eggs and scramble till the eggs are done. Serve hot.

Chicken Curry with Dry Coconut

Serves 4

Ingredients

1kg/2¼lb chicken, chopped into 12 pieces

Salt to taste

Juice of half a lemon

1 large onion, sliced

4 tbsp desiccated coconut

1 tsp turmeric

8 garlic cloves

2.5cm/1in root ginger

½ tsp fennel seeds

1 tsp garam masala

1 tsp poppy seeds

4 tbsp refined vegetable oil

500ml/16fl oz water

Method

- Marinate the chicken with the salt and lemon juice for 30 minutes.

- Dry roast the onion and coconut for 5 minutes.

- Mix with all the remaining ingredients, except the oil and water. Grind with enough water to form a smooth paste.

- Heat the oil in a saucepan. Add the paste and fry on a low heat for 7-8 minutes. Add the chicken and water. Simmer for 40 minutes. Serve hot.

Simple Chicken

Serves 4

Ingredients

1kg/2¼lb chicken, chopped into 8 pieces

Salt to taste

1 tsp chilli powder

½ tsp turmeric

3 tbsp refined vegetable oil

2 large onions, finely sliced

1 tsp ginger paste

1 tsp garlic paste

4-5 whole red chillies, deseeded

4 small tomatoes, finely chopped

1 tbsp garam masala

250ml/8fl oz water

Method

- Marinate the chicken with the salt, chilli powder and turmeric for 1 hour.

- Heat the oil in a saucepan. Add the onions and fry on a medium heat till brown. Add the ginger paste and garlic paste. Fry for 1 minute.

- Add the marinated chicken and the remaining ingredients. Mix well. Cover with a lid and simmer for 40 minutes. Serve hot.

Southern Chicken Curry

Serves 4

Ingredients

1 tsp ginger paste

1 tsp garlic paste

2 green chillies, finely chopped

1 tsp lemon juice

Salt to taste

1kg/2¼lb chicken, chopped into 10 pieces

3 tbsp refined vegetable oil

2.5cm/1in cinnamon

3 green cardamom pods

3 cloves

1 star anise

2 bay leaves

3 large onions, finely chopped

½ tsp chilli powder

½ tsp turmeric

1 tbsp ground coriander

250ml/8fl oz coconut milk

For the seasoning:

½ tsp mustard seeds

8 curry leaves

3 whole dry red chillies

Method

- Mix the ginger paste, garlic paste, green chillies, lemon juice and salt together. Marinate the chicken with this mixture for 30 minutes.

- Heat half the oil in a saucepan. Add the cinnamon, cardamom, cloves, star anise and bay leaves. Let them splutter for 30 seconds.

- Add the onions and fry them on a medium heat till they turn brown.

- Add the marinated chicken, chilli powder, turmeric and ground coriander. Mix well and cover with a lid. Cook on a low heat for 20 minutes.

- Add the coconut milk. Mix well and cook for 10 more minutes, stirring frequently. Set aside.

- Heat the remaining oil in a small saucepan. Add the seasoning ingredients. Let them splutter for 30 seconds.

- Pour this seasoning in the chicken curry. Mix well and serve hot.

Chicken Stew in Coconut Milk

Serves 4

Ingredients

2 tbsp refined vegetable oil

2 onions, chopped into 8 pieces each

1 tsp ginger paste

1 tsp garlic paste

3 green chillies, slit lengthways

2 tbsp garam masala

8 chicken drumsticks

750ml/1¼ pints coconut milk

200g/7oz frozen mixed vegetables

Salt to taste

2 tsp rice flour, dissolved in 120ml/4fl oz water

Method

- Heat the oil in a saucepan. Add the onions, ginger paste, garlic paste, green chillies and garam masala. Fry for 5 minutes, stirring constantly.

- Add the drumsticks and coconut milk. Mix well. Simmer for 20 minutes.

- Add the vegetables and salt. Mix well and cook for 15 minutes.

- Add the rice flour mixture. Simmer for 5-10 minutes and serve hot.

Chandi Tikka

(Fried Chicken Pieces coated with Oatmeal)

Serves 4

Ingredients

1 tbsp lemon juice

1 tsp ginger paste

1 tsp garlic paste

75g/2½oz Cheddar cheese

200g/7oz yoghurt

¾ tsp ground white pepper

1 tsp black cumin seeds

Salt to taste

4 chicken breasts

1 egg, whisked

45g/1½oz oatmeal

Method

- Mix together all the ingredients, except the chicken breasts, egg and oatmeal. Marinate the chicken with this mixture for 3-4 hours.

- Dip the marinated chicken breasts in the egg, coat with the oatmeal and grill for an hour, turning occasionally. Serve hot.

Tandoori Chicken

Serves 4

Ingredients

1 tbsp lemon juice

2 tsp ginger paste

2 tsp garlic paste

2 green chillies, finely grated

1 tbsp coriander leaves, ground

1 tsp chilli powder

1 tbsp garam masala

1 tbsp ground raw papaya

½ tsp orange food colour

1½ tbsp refined vegetable oil

Salt to taste

1kg/2¼lb whole chicken

Method

- Mix together all the ingredients, except the chicken. Make incisions on the chicken and marinate it with this mixture for 6-8 hours.

- Roast the chicken in an oven at 200°C (400°F, Gas Mark 6) for 40 minutes. Serve hot.

Murgh Lajawab

(Chicken cooked with Rich Indian Spices)

Serves 4

Ingredients

1kg/2¼lb chicken, chopped into 8 pieces 1 tsp ginger paste

1 tsp garlic paste

4 tbsp ghee

2 tsp poppy seeds, ground

1 tsp melon seeds*, ground

6 almonds

3 green cardamom pods

¼ tsp ground nutmeg

1 tsp garam masala

2 pieces mace

Salt to taste

750ml/1¼ pints milk

6 strands saffron

Method

- Marinate the chicken with the ginger paste and garlic paste for an hour.

- Heat the ghee in a saucepan and fry the marinated chicken for 10 minutes on a medium heat.

- Add all the remaining ingredients except the milk and saffron. Mix well, cover with a lid and simmer for 20 minutes.

- Add the milk and saffron and simmer for 10 minutes. Serve hot.

Lahori Chicken

(North-West Frontier-style Chicken)

Serves 4

Ingredients

50g/1¾oz yoghurt

1 tsp ginger paste

1 tsp garlic paste

1 tsp chilli powder

½ tsp turmeric

1kg/2¼lb chicken, chopped into 12 pieces

4 tbsp refined vegetable oil

2 large onions, finely chopped

1 tsp sesame seeds, ground

1 tsp poppy seeds, ground

10 cashew nuts, ground

2 large green peppers, deseeded and finely chopped

500ml/16fl oz coconut milk

Salt to taste

Method

- Mix together the yoghurt, ginger paste, garlic paste, chilli powder and turmeric. Marinate the chicken with this mixture for 1 hour.

- Heat the oil in a saucepan. Fry the onions on a low heat till brown.

- Add the marinated chicken. Fry for 7-8 minutes. Add all the remaining ingredients and cook for 30 minutes, stirring occasionally. Serve hot.

Chicken Liver

Serves 4

Ingredients

3 tbsp refined vegetable oil

2 large onions, finely sliced

5 garlic cloves, minced

8 chicken livers

1 tsp ground black pepper

1 tsp lemon juice

Salt to taste

Method

- Heat the oil in a saucepan. Add the onions and garlic. Fry on a medium heat for 3-4 minutes.

- Add all the remaining ingredients. Fry for 15-20 minutes, stirring occasionally. Serve hot.

Balti Chicken

Serves 4

Ingredients

4 tbsp ghee

1 tsp turmeric

1 tbsp mustard seeds

1 tbsp cumin seeds

8 garlic cloves, finely chopped

2.5cm/1in root ginger, finely chopped

3 small onions, finely chopped

7 green chillies

750g/1lb 10oz chicken breast, chopped

1 tbsp ground coriander

1 tbsp single cream

1 tsp garam masala

Salt to taste

Method

- Heat the ghee in a saucepan. Add the turmeric, mustard seeds and cumin seeds. Let them splutter for 30 seconds. Add the garlic, ginger, onions and green chillies and fry on a medium heat for 2-3 minutes.

- Add all the remaining ingredients. Cook on a low heat for 30 minutes, stirring occasionally. Serve hot.

Tangy Chicken

Serves 4

Ingredients

8 chicken drumsticks

2 tsp green chilli sauce

2 tbsp refined vegetable oil

2 large onions, finely sliced

10 garlic cloves, finely chopped

Salt to taste

Pinch of sugar

2 tsp malt vinegar

Method

- Marinate the chicken with the chilli sauce for 30 minutes.

- Heat the oil in a saucepan. Add the onions and fry on a medium heat till translucent.

- Add the garlic, marinated chicken and salt. Mix well and cook on a low heat for 30 minutes, stirring occasionally.

- Add the sugar and vinegar. Mix thoroughly and serve hot.

Chicken Dilruba

(Chicken in Rich Gravy)

Serves 4

Ingredients

5 tbsp refined vegetable oil

20 almonds, ground

20 cashew nuts, ground

2 small onions, ground

5cm/2in root ginger, grated

1kg/2¼lb chicken, chopped into 8 pieces

200g/7oz yoghurt

240ml/6fl oz milk

1 tsp garam masala

½ tsp turmeric

1 tsp chilli powder

Salt to taste

1 pinch saffron, soaked in 1 tbsp milk

2 tbsp coriander leaves, chopped

Method

- Heat the oil in a saucepan. Add the almonds, cashew nuts, onions and ginger. Fry on a medium heat for 3 minutes.

- Add the chicken and yoghurt. Mix well and cook on a medium heat for 20 minutes.

- Add the milk, garam masala, turmeric, chilli powder and salt. Mix well. Cover with a lid and cook on a low heat for 20 minutes.

- Garnish with the saffron and coriander leaves. Serve hot.

Fried Chicken Wings

Serves 4

Ingredients

¼ tsp turmeric

1 tsp garam masala

1 tsp chaat masala*

Salt to taste

1 egg, whisked

Refined vegetable oil for deep frying

12 chicken wings

Method

- Mix together the turmeric, garam masala, chaat masala, salt and egg to make a smooth batter.

- Heat the oil in a frying pan. Dip the chicken wings in the batter and deep fry on a medium heat till golden brown.

- Drain on absorbent paper and serve hot.

Murgh Mussalam

(Stuffed Chicken)

Serves 6

Ingredients

2 tbsp ghee

2 large onions, grated

4 black cardamom pods, ground

1 tsp poppy seeds

50g/1¾oz desiccated coconut

1 tsp mace

1kg/2¼lb chicken

4-5 tbsp besan*

2-3 bay leaves

6-7 green cardamom pods

3 tsp garlic paste

200g/7oz yoghurt

Salt to taste

Method

- Heat ½ tbsp ghee in a saucepan. Add the onions and fry till brown.

- Add the cardamom, poppy seeds, coconut and mace. Fry for 3 minutes.

- Stuff the chicken with this mixture and sew up the opening. Set aside.

- Heat the remaining ghee in a saucepan. Add all the remaining ingredients and the chicken. Simmer for 1½ hours, stirring occasionally. Serve hot.

Chicken Delight

Serves 4

Ingredients

4 tbsp refined vegetable oil

5cm/2in ground cinnamon

1 tbsp cardamom powder

8 ground cloves

½ tsp grated nutmeg

2 large onions, ground

10 garlic cloves, crushed

2.5cm/1in root ginger, grated

Salt to taste

1kg/2¼lb chicken, chopped into 8 pieces

200g/7oz yoghurt

300g/10oz tomato purée

Method

- Heat the oil in a saucepan. Add the cinnamon, cardamom, cloves, nutmeg, onions, garlic and ginger. Fry on a medium heat for 5 minutes.

- Add the salt, chicken, yoghurt and tomato purée. Mix well and simmer for 40 minutes, stirring frequently. Serve hot.

Salli Chicken

(Chicken with Potato Crisps)

Serves 4

Ingredients

Salt to taste

1 tsp ginger paste

1 tsp garlic paste

1kg/2¼lb chicken, chopped

3 tbsp refined vegetable oil

2 large onions, finely chopped

1 tsp sugar

4 tomatoes, puréed

1 tsp turmeric

250g/9oz plain salted potato crisps

Method

- Mix together the salt, ginger paste and garlic paste. Marinate the chicken with this mixture for 1 hour. Set aside.

- Heat the oil in a saucepan. Fry the onions on a low heat till brown.

- Add the marinated chicken and the sugar, tomato purée and turmeric. Cover with a lid and simmer for 40 minutes, stirring frequently.

- Sprinkle the potato crisps on top and serve hot.

Fried Chicken Tikka

Serves 4

Ingredients

1kg/2¼lb boneless chicken, chopped

1 litre/1¾ pints milk

1 tsp saffron

8 green cardamom pods

5 cloves

2.5cm/1in cinnamon

2 bay leaves

250g/9oz Basmati rice

4 tsp fennel seeds

Salt to taste

150g/5½oz yoghurt

Refined vegetable oil for deep-frying

Method

- Mix the chicken with the milk, saffron, cardamom, cloves, cinnamon and bay leaves. Cook in a saucepan on a low heat for 50 minutes. Set aside.

- Grind the rice with the fennel seeds, salt and enough water to form a fine paste. Add this paste to the yoghurt and whisk thoroughly.

- Heat the oil in a frying pan. Dip the chicken pieces in the yoghurt mixture and fry on a medium heat till golden brown. Serve hot.

Chicken Seekh

Serves 4

Ingredients

500g/1lb 2oz chicken, minced

10 garlic cloves, ground

5cm/2in root ginger, julienned

2 green chillies, finely chopped

½ tsp black cumin seeds

Salt to taste

Method

- Mix the mince with all the ingredients and knead into a smooth dough. Divide this mixture into 8 equal portions.

- Skewer and grill for 10 minutes.

- Serve hot with mint chutney

Nadan Kozhikari

(Chicken with Fennel and Coconut Milk)

Serves 4

Ingredients

½ tsp turmeric

2 tsp ginger paste

Salt to taste

1kg/2¼lb chicken, chopped into 8 pieces

1 tbsp coriander seeds

3 red chillies

1 tsp fennel seeds

1 tsp mustard seeds

3 large onions

3 tbsp refined vegetable oil

750ml/1¼ pints coconut milk

250ml/8fl oz water

10 curry leaves

Method

- Mix the turmeric, ginger paste and salt for 1 hour. Marinate the chicken with this mixture for 1 hour.

- Dry roast the coriander seeds, red chillies, fennel seeds and mustard seeds. Mix with the onions and grind to a smooth paste.

- Heat the oil in a saucepan. Add the onion paste and fry on a low heat for 7 minutes. Add the marinated chicken, coconut milk and water. Simmer for 40 minutes. Serve garnished with the curry leaves.

Mum's Chicken

Serves 4

Ingredients

3 tbsp refined vegetable oil

5cm/2in cinnamon

2 green cardamom pods

4 cloves

4 large onions, finely chopped

2.5cm/1in root ginger, grated

8 garlic cloves, crushed

3 large tomatoes, finely chopped

2 tsp ground coriander

1 tsp turmeric

Salt to taste

1kg/2¼lb chicken, chopped into 12 pieces

500ml/16fl oz water

Method

- Heat the oil in a saucepan. Add the cinnamon, cardamom and cloves. Let them splutter for 15 seconds.
- Add the onions, ginger and garlic. Fry on a medium heat for 2 minutes.
- Add the remaining ingredients, except the water. Fry for 5 minutes.
- Pour in the water. Mix well and simmer for 40 minutes. Serve hot.

Methi Chicken

(Chicken cooked with Fenugreek Leaves)

Serves 4

Ingredients

1 tsp ginger paste

2 tsp garlic paste

2 tsp ground coriander

½ tsp ground cloves

Juice of 1 lemon

1kg/2¼lb chicken, chopped into 8 pieces

4 tsp butter

1 tsp dry ginger powder

2 tbsp dried fenugreek leaves

50g/1¾oz coriander leaves, chopped

10g/¼oz mint leaves, finely chopped

Salt to taste

Method

- Mix the ginger paste, garlic paste, ground coriander, cloves and half the lemon juice. Marinate the chicken with this mixture for 2 hours.
- Bake in an oven at 200°C (400°F, Gas Mark 6) for 50 minutes. Set aside.
- Heat the butter in a saucepan. Add the roasted chicken and all the remaining ingredients. Toss well. Cook for 5-6 minutes and serve hot.

Spicy Chicken Drumsticks

Serves 4

Ingredients

8-10 chicken drumsticks, pricked all over with a fork

2 eggs, whisked

100g/3½oz semolina

Refined vegetable oil for deep-frying

For the spice mixture:

6 red chillies

6 garlic cloves

2.5cm/1in root ginger

1 tbsp coriander leaves, chopped

6 cloves

15 black peppercorns

Salt to taste

4 tbsp malt vinegar

Method

- Grind the ingredients for the spice mixture to a smooth paste. Marinate the drumsticks with this paste for an hour.
- Heat the oil in a frying pan. Dip the drumsticks in the egg, roll in the semolina and fry on a medium heat till golden brown. Serve hot.

Dieter's Chicken Curry

Serves 4

Ingredients

1 tsp ginger paste

1 tsp garlic paste

200g/7oz yoghurt

1 tsp chilli powder

½ tsp turmeric

2 tomatoes, finely chopped

1 tsp ground coriander

1 tsp ground cumin

1 tsp dried fenugreek leaves, crushed

2 tsp garam masala

1 tsp mango pickle

Salt to taste

750g/1lb 10oz chicken, chopped

Method

- Mix together all the ingredients, except the chicken. Marinate the chicken with this mixture for 3 hours.
- Cook the mixture in an earthenware pot or a saucepan on a low heat for 40 minutes. Add water if required. Serve hot.

Heavenly Chicken

Serves 4

Ingredients

4 tbsp refined vegetable oil

1kg/2¼lb chicken, chopped into 8 pieces

Salt to taste

1 tsp pepper

1 tsp turmeric

6 spring onions, finely chopped

250ml/8fl oz water

For the spice mixture:

1½ tsp ginger paste

1½ tsp garlic paste

3 green peppers, deseeded and sliced

2 green chillies

½ fresh coconut, grated

2 tomatoes, finely chopped

Method

- Grind together the spice mixture ingredients into a smooth paste.
- Heat the oil in a saucepan. Add the paste and fry on a low heat for 7 minutes. Add the remaining ingredients, except the water. Fry for 5 minutes. Add the water. Mix well and simmer for 40 minutes. Serve hot.

Chicken Rizala

Serves 4

Ingredients

6 tbsp refined vegetable oil

2 large onions, sliced lengthways

1 tsp ginger paste

1 tsp garlic paste

2 tbsp poppy seeds, ground

1 tbsp ground coriander

2 large green peppers, julienned

360ml/12fl oz water

1kg/2¼lb chicken, chopped into 8 pieces

6 green cardamom pods

5 cloves

200g/7oz yoghurt

1 tsp garam masala

Juice of 1 lemon

Salt to taste

Method

- Heat the oil in a saucepan. Add the onions, ginger paste, garlic paste, poppy seeds and ground coriander. Fry on a low heat for 2 minutes.
- Add all the remaining ingredients and mix well. Cover with a lid and simmer for 40 minutes, stirring occasionally. Serve hot.

Chicken Surprise

Serves 4

Ingredients

150g/5½oz coriander leaves, chopped

10 garlic cloves

2.5cm/1in root ginger

1 tsp garam masala

1 tbsp tamarind paste

2 tsp cumin seeds

1 tsp turmeric

4 tbsp water

Salt to taste

1kg/2¼lb chicken, chopped into 8 pieces

Refined vegetable oil for deep-frying

2 eggs, whisked

Method

- Grind all the ingredients, except the chicken, oil and eggs, into a smooth paste. Marinate the chicken with this paste for 2 hours.
- Heat the oil in a frying pan. Dip each chicken piece in the eggs and deep fry on a medium heat till brown. Serve hot.

Cheesy Chicken

Serves 4

Ingredients

12 chicken drumsticks

4 tbsp butter

1 tsp ginger paste

1 tsp garlic paste

2 large onions, finely chopped

1 tsp garam masala

Salt to taste

200g/7oz yoghurt

For the marinade:

1 tsp ginger paste

1 tsp garlic paste

1 tbsp lemon juice

¼ tsp garam masala

4 tbsp single cream

4 tbsp Cheddar cheese, grated

Salt to taste

Method

- Pierce the drumsticks all over with a fork. Mix together all the marinade ingredients. Marinate the drumsticks with this mixture for 8-10 hours.
- Heat the butter in a saucepan. Add the ginger paste and garlic paste. Fry on a medium heat for 1-2 minutes. Add all the remaining ingredients, except the yoghurt. Fry for 5 minutes.
- Add the drumsticks and the yoghurt. Simmer for 40 minutes. Serve hot.

Beef Korma

(Beef cooked in a Spicy Gravy)

Serves 4

Ingredients

4 tbsp refined vegetable oil

2 large onions, finely chopped

675g/1½lb beef, chopped into 2.5cm/1in pieces

360ml/12fl oz water

½ tsp ground cinnamon

120ml/4fl oz single cream

125g/4½oz yoghurt

1 tsp garam masala

Salt to taste

10g/¼oz coriander leaves, finely chopped

For the spice mixture:

1½ tbsp coriander seeds

¾ tbsp cumin seeds

3 green cardamom pods

4 black peppercorns

6 cloves

2.5cm/1in root ginger

10 garlic cloves

15 almonds

Method

- Mix all the ingredients of the spice mixture together and grind with enough water to form a smooth paste. Set aside.
- Heat the oil in a saucepan. Add the onions and fry them on a medium heat till they turn brown.
- Add the spice mixture paste and the beef. Fry for 2-3 minutes. Add the water. Mix well and simmer for 45 minutes.
- Add the ground cinnamon, cream, yoghurt, garam masala and salt. Stir thoroughly for 3-4 minutes.
- Garnish the beef korma with the coriander leaves. Serve hot.

Dhal Kheema

(Mince with Lentils)

Serves 4

Ingredients

675g/1½lb lamb, minced

1 tsp ginger paste

1 tsp garlic paste

3 large onions, finely chopped

360ml/12fl oz water

Salt to taste

600g/1lb 5oz chana dhal*, soaked in 250ml/8fl oz water for 30 minutes

½ tsp tamarind paste

60ml/2fl oz refined vegetable oil

4 cloves

2.5cm/1in cinnamon

2 green cardamom pods

4 black peppercorns

10g/¼oz coriander leaves, finely chopped

For the spice mixture:

2 tsp coriander seeds

3 red chillies

½ tsp turmeric

¼ tsp cumin seeds

25g/scant 1oz fresh coconut, grated

1 tsp poppy seeds

Method

- Dry roast all the ingredients of the spice mixture together. Grind this mixture with enough water to form a smooth paste. Set aside.
- Mix the minced lamb with the ginger paste, garlic paste, half the onions, the remaining water and the salt. Cook in a saucepan on a medium heat for 40 minutes.
- Add the chana dhal along with the water in which it was soaked. Mix well. Simmer for 10 minutes.
- Add the spice mixture paste and the tamarind paste. Cover with a lid and simmer for 10 minutes, stirring occasionally. Set aside.
- Heat the oil in a frying pan. Add the remaining onions and fry them on a medium heat till they turn brown.
- Add the cloves, cinnamon, cardamom and peppercorns. Fry for a minute.
- Remove from the heat and pour this directly over the mince-dhal mixture. Stir thoroughly for a minute.
- Garnish the dhal kheema with the coriander leaves. Serve hot.

Pork Curry

Serves 4

Ingredients

500g/1lb 2oz pork, chopped into 2.5cm/1in pieces

1 tbsp malt vinegar

6 curry leaves

2.5cm/1in cinnamon

3 cloves

500ml/16fl oz water

Salt to taste

2 large potatoes, diced

3 tbsp refined vegetable oil

1 tsp garam masala

For the spice mixture:

1 tbsp coriander seeds

1 tsp cumin seeds

6 black peppercorns

½ tsp turmeric

4 red chillies

2 large onions, finely chopped

2.5cm/1in root ginger, sliced

10 garlic cloves, sliced

½ tsp tamarind paste

Method

- Mix all the ingredients for the spice mixture together. Grind with enough water to form a smooth paste. Set aside.
- Mix the pork with the vinegar, curry leaves, cinnamon, cloves, water and the salt. Cook this mixture in a saucepan on a medium heat for 40 minutes.
- Add the potatoes. Mix well and simmer for 10 minutes. Set aside.
- Heat the oil in a saucepan. Add the spice mixture paste and fry it on a medium heat for 3-4 minutes.
- Add the pork mixture and the garam masala. Mix well. Cover with a lid and simmer for 10 minutes, stirring occasionally.
- Serve hot.

Shikampoore Kebab

(Lamb Kebab)

Serves 4

Ingredients

3 large onions

8 garlic cloves

2.5cm/1in root ginger

6 dry red chillies

4 tbsp ghee plus extra for frying

1 tsp turmeric

1 tsp ground coriander

½ tsp ground cumin

10 almonds, ground

10 pistachios, ground

1 tsp garam masala

Pinch of ground cinnamon

1 tbsp ground cloves

1 tbsp ground green cardamom

2 tbsp coconut milk

Salt to taste

1 tbsp besan*

750g/1lb 10oz lamb, minced

200g/7oz Greek yoghurt

1 tbsp mint leaves, finely chopped

Method

- Mix together the onions, garlic, ginger and chillies.
- Grind this mixture with enough water to form a smooth paste.
- Heat the ghee in a saucepan. Add this paste and fry it on a medium heat for 1-2 minutes.
- Add the turmeric, ground coriander and ground cumin. Fry for a minute.
- Add the ground almonds, ground pistachios, garam masala, ground cinnamon, ground cloves and cardamom. Continue to fry for 2-3 minutes.
- Add the coconut milk and salt. Mix well. Stir for 5 minutes.
- Add the besan and the mince. Mix well. Simmer for 30 minutes, stirring occasionally. Remove from the heat and set aside to cool for 10 minutes.
- Once the mince mixture is cool, divide it into 8 balls and flatten each into a cutlet. Set aside.

- Whisk the yoghurt thoroughly with the mint leaves. Place a large spoonful of this mixture in the centre of each flattened cutlet. Seal like a pouch, roll into a ball and flatten again.
- Heat the ghee in a frying pan. Add the cutlets and deep fry them on a medium heat till golden brown. Serve hot.

Special Mutton

Serves 4

Ingredients

5 tbsp ghee

4 large onions, sliced

2 tomatoes, sliced

675g/1½lb mutton, chopped into 3.5cm/1½in pieces

1 litre/1¾ pints water

Salt to taste

For the spice mixture:

10 garlic cloves

3 green chillies

3.5cm/1½in root ginger

4 cloves

2.5cm/1in cinnamon

1 tbsp poppy seeds

1 tsp black cumin seeds

1 tsp cumin seeds

2 green cardamom pods

2 tbsp coriander seeds

7 peppercorns

5 dry red chillies

1 tsp turmeric

1 tbsp chana dhal*

25g/scant 1oz mint leaves

25g/scant 1oz coriander leaves

100g/3½oz fresh coconut, grated

Method

- Mix all the spice mixture ingredients together and grind with enough water to form a smooth paste. Set aside.
- Heat the ghee in a saucepan. Add the onions and fry them on a medium heat till they turn brown.
- Add the spice mixture paste. Fry for 3-4 minutes, stirring occasionally.
- Add the tomatoes and mutton. Fry for 8-10 minutes. Add the water and salt. Mix well, cover with a lid and simmer for 45 minutes, stirring occasionally. Serve hot.

Green Masala Chops

Serves 4

Ingredients

750g/1lb 10oz mutton chops

Salt to taste

360ml/12fl oz refined vegetable oil

3 large potatoes, sliced

5cm/2in cinnamon

2 green cardamom pods

4 cloves

3 tomatoes, finely chopped

¼ tsp turmeric

120ml/4fl oz vinegar

250ml/8fl oz water

For the spice mixture:

3 large onions

2.5cm/1in root ginger

10-12 garlic cloves

¼ tsp cumin seeds

6 green chillies, slit lengthways

1 tsp coriander seeds

1 tsp cumin seeds

50g/1¾oz coriander leaves, finely chopped

Method

- Marinate the mutton with the salt for an hour.
- Mix all the spice mixture ingredients together. Grind with enough water to form a smooth paste. Set aside.
- Heat half the oil in a frying pan. Add the potatoes and fry them on a medium heat till they turn golden brown. Drain and set aside.
- Heat the remaining oil in a saucepan. Add the cinnamon, cardamom and cloves. Let them splutter for 20 seconds.
- Add the spice mixture paste. Fry it on a medium heat for 3-4 minutes.
- Add the tomatoes and turmeric. Continue to fry for 1-2 minutes.
- Add the vinegar and the marinated mutton. Fry for 6-7 minutes.
- Add the water and mix well. Cover with a lid and simmer for 45 minutes, stirring occasionally.
- Add the fried potatoes. Cook for 5 minutes, stirring continuously. Serve hot.

Layered Kebab

Serves 4

Ingredients

120ml/4fl oz refined vegetable oil

100g/3½oz breadcrumbs

For the white layer:

450g/1lb goat's cheese, drained

1 large potato, boiled

½ tsp salt

½ tsp ground black pepper

½ tsp chilli powder

Juice of half a lemon

50g/1¾oz coriander leaves, chopped

For the green layer:

200g/7oz spinach

2 tbsp mung dhal*

1 large onion, finely chopped

2.5cm/1in root ginger

4 cloves

¼ tsp turmeric

1 tsp garam masala

Salt to taste

250ml/8fl oz water

2 tbsp besan*

For the orange layer:

1 egg, whisked

1 large onion, finely chopped

1 tbsp lemon juice

¼ tsp orange food colouring

For the meat layer:

500g/1lb 2oz meat, minced

150g/5½oz mung dhal*, soaked for 1 hour

5cm/2in root ginger

6 garlic cloves

6 cloves

1 tbsp ground cumin

1 tbsp chilli powder

10 black peppercorns

600ml/1 pint water

Method

- Mix and knead the white layer ingredients with some salt. Set aside.

- Mix together all the green layer ingredients, except the besan. Cook in a saucepan on a low heat for 45 minutes. Mash with the besan and set aside.
- Mix all the ingredients for the orange layer with some salt. Set aside.
- For the meat layer, mix all the ingredients with some salt and cook in a saucepan on a medium heat for 40 minutes. Cool and mash.
- Divide each layer mixture into 8 portions. Roll into balls and pat lightly to form cutlets. Place 1 cutlet of each layer over the other, so you have eight 4-layer patties. Press lightly into oblong-shaped kebabs.
- Heat the oil in a frying pan. Roll the kebabs in the breadcrumbs and deep fry them on a medium heat till they turn golden brown. Serve hot.

Barrah Champ

(Roasted Lamb Chops)

Serves 4

Ingredients

1 tsp ginger paste

1 tsp garlic paste

3 tbsp malt vinegar

675g/1½lb lamb chops

400g/14oz Greek yoghurt

1 tsp turmeric

4 green chillies, finely chopped

½ tsp chilli powder

1 tsp ground coriander

1 tsp ground cumin

1 tsp ground cinnamon

¾ tsp ground cloves

Salt to taste

1 tbsp chaat masala*

Method

- Mix the ginger paste and garlic paste with the vinegar. Marinate the lamb with this mixture for 2 hours.
- Mix together all the remaining ingredients, except the chaat masala. Marinate the lamb chops with this mixture for 4 hours.
- Skewer the chops and roast in an oven at 200°C (400°F, Gas Mark 6) for 40 minutes.
- Garnish with the chaat masala and serve hot.

Lamb Pickle

Serves 4

Ingredients

10 red dry chillies

10 garlic cloves

3.5cm/1½in root ginger

Salt to taste

750ml/1¼ pints water

2 tbsp yoghurt

675g/1½lb lamb, chopped into 2.5cm/1in pieces

250ml/8fl oz refined vegetable oil

1½ tsp turmeric

1 tbsp coriander seeds

10 black peppercorns

3 black cardamom pods

4 cloves

3 bay leaves

1 tsp grated mace

¼ tsp grated nutmeg

1 tsp cumin seeds

½ tsp mustard seeds

100g/3½oz desiccated coconut

½ tsp asafoetida

Juice of 1 lemon

Method

- Mix together the red chillies, garlic, ginger and salt together. Grind with enough water to form a smooth paste.
- Mix this paste with the yoghurt. Marinate the meat with this mixture for 1 hour.
- Heat half the oil in a saucepan. Add the turmeric, coriander seeds, peppercorns, cardamom, cloves, bay leaves, mace, nutmeg, cumin seeds, mustards seeds and coconut. Fry on a medium heat for 2-3 minutes.
- Grind the mixture with enough water to form a thick paste.
- Add the remaining oil in a saucepan. Add the asafoetida. Let it splutter for 10 seconds.
- Add the ground turmeric-coriander seeds paste. Fry on a medium heat for 3-4 minutes.
- Add the marinated lamb and the remaining water. Mix well. Cover with a lid and simmer for 45 minutes. Set aside to cool.
- Add the lemon juice and mix thoroughly. Store the lamb pickle in an airtight container.

Goan Lamb Curry

Serves 4

Ingredients

240ml/6fl oz refined vegetable oil

4 large onions, finely chopped

1 tsp turmeric

4 tomatoes, puréed

675g/1½lb lamb, chopped into 2.5cm/1in pieces

4 large potatoes, diced

600ml/1 pint coconut milk

120ml/4fl oz water

Salt to taste

For the spice mixture:

4 green cardamom pods

5cm/2in cinnamon

6 black peppercorns

1 tsp cumin seeds

2 cloves

6 red chillies

1 star anise

50g/1¾oz coriander leaves, finely chopped

3 green chillies

1 tsp ginger paste

1 tsp garlic paste

Method

- To prepare the spice mixture, dry roast the cardamom, cinnamon, peppercorns, cumin seeds, cloves, red chillies and star anise for 3-4 minutes.
- Grind this mixture with the remaining spice mixture ingredients and enough water to form a smooth paste. Set aside.
- Heat the oil in a saucepan. Add the onions and fry them on a medium heat till they turn translucent.
- Add the turmeric and tomato purée. Fry for 2 minutes.
- Add the spice mixture paste. Continue to fry for 4-5 minutes.
- Add the lamb and potatoes. Fry for 5-6 minutes.
- Add the coconut milk, water and salt. Mix well. Cover with a lid and cook the mixture on a low heat for 45 minutes, stirring occasionally. Serve hot.

Bagara Meat

(Meat cooked in Rich Indian Gravy)

Serves 4

Ingredients

120ml/4fl oz refined vegetable oil

3 red chillies

1 tsp cumin seeds

10 curry leaves

2 large onions

½ tsp turmeric

1 tsp chilli powder

1 tsp ground coriander

1 tsp tamarind paste

1 tsp garam masala

500g/1lb 2oz mutton, diced

Salt to taste

500ml/16fl oz water

For the spice mixture:

2 tbsp sesame seeds

2 tbsp fresh coconut, grated

2 tbsp peanuts

2.5cm/1in root ginger

8 garlic cloves

Method

- Mix the ingredients for the spice mixture together. Grind this mixture with enough water to form a smooth paste. Set aside.
- Heat the oil in a saucepan. Add the red chillies, cumin seeds and curry leaves. Let them splutter for 15 seconds.
- Add the onions and the spice mixture paste. Fry on a medium heat for 4-5 minutes.
- Add the remaining ingredients, except the water. Fry for 5-6 minutes.
- Add the water. Mix well. Cover with a lid and simmer for 45 minutes. Serve hot.

Liver in Coconut Milk

Serves 4

Ingredients

750g/1lb 10oz liver, chopped into 2.5cm/1in pieces

½ tsp turmeric

Salt to taste

500ml/16fl oz water

5 tbsp refined vegetable oil

3 large onions, finely chopped

1 tbsp ginger, finely chopped

1 tbsp garlic cloves, finely chopped

6 green chillies, slit lengthways

3 large potatoes, chopped into 2.5cm/1in pieces

1 tbsp malt vinegar

500ml/16fl oz coconut milk

For the spice mixture:

3 dry red chillies

2.5cm/1in cinnamon

4 green cardamom pods

1 tsp cumin seeds

8 black peppercorns

Method

- Mix the liver with the turmeric, salt and water. Cook in a saucepan on a medium heat for 40 minutes. Set aside.
- Mix all the spice mixture ingredients together and grind with enough water to form a smooth paste. Set aside.
- Heat the oil in a saucepan. Add the onions and fry them on a medium heat till they turn translucent.
- Add the ginger, garlic and green chillies. Fry for 2 minutes.
- Add the spice mixture paste. Continue to fry for 1-2 minutes.
- Add the liver mixture, potatoes, vinegar and the coconut milk. Stir thoroughly for 2 minutes. Cover with a lid and simmer for 15 minutes, stirring occasionally. Serve hot.

Lamb Masala with Yoghurt

Serves 4

Ingredients

200g/7oz yoghurt

Salt to taste

675g/1½lb lamb, chopped into 2.5cm/1in pieces

4 tbsp refined vegetable oil

3 large onions, finely chopped

3 carrots, diced

3 tomatoes, finely chopped

120ml/4fl oz water

For the spice mixture:

25g/scant 1oz coriander leaves, finely chopped

¼ tsp turmeric

2.5cm/1in root ginger

2 green chillies

8 garlic cloves

4 cardamom pods

4 cloves

5cm/2in cinnamon

3 curry leaves

¾ tsp turmeric

2 tsp ground coriander

1 tsp chilli powder

½ tsp tamarind paste

Method

- Mix all the spice mixture ingredients together. Grind with enough water to form a smooth paste.
- Mix the paste thoroughly with the yoghurt and salt. Marinate the lamb with this mixture for 1 hour.
- Heat the oil in a saucepan. Add the onions and fry them on a medium heat till they turn translucent.
- Add the carrots and tomatoes and fry for 3-4 minutes.
- Add the marinated lamb and the water. Mix well. Cover with a lid and simmer for 45 minutes, stirring occasionally. Serve hot.

Korma in Khada Masala

(Spicy Lamb in Thick Gravy)

Serves 4

Ingredients

75g/2½oz ghee

3 black cardamom pods

6 cloves

2 bay leaves

½ tsp cumin seeds

2 large onions, sliced

3 dry red chillies

2.5cm/1in root ginger, finely chopped

20 garlic cloves

5 green chillies, slit lengthways

675g/1½lb mutton, diced

½ tsp chilli powder

2 tsp ground coriander

6-8 shallots, peeled

200g/7oz canned peas

750 ml/1¼fl oz water

Pinch of saffron, dissolved in 2 tbsp warm water

Salt to taste

1 tsp lemon juice

200g/7oz yoghurt

1 tbsp coriander leaves, finely chopped

4 hard-boiled eggs, halved

Method

- Heat the ghee in a saucepan. Add the cardamom, cloves, bay leaves and cumin seeds. Let them splutter for 30 seconds.
- Add the onions and fry them on a medium heat till they turn brown.
- Add the dry red chillies, ginger, garlic and green chillies. Fry for a minute.
- Add the mutton. Fry for 5-6 minutes.
- Add the chilli powder, ground coriander, shallots and peas. Continue to fry for 3-4 minutes.
- Add the water, saffron mixture, salt and lemon juice. Stir thoroughly for 2-3 minutes. Cover with a lid and simmer for 20 minutes.
- Uncover the pan and add the yoghurt. Mix well. Cover again and continue to simmer for 20-25 minutes, stirring occasionally.
- Garnish with the coriander leaves and eggs. Serve hot.

Lamb & Kidney Curry

Serves 4

Ingredients

5 tbsp refined vegetable oil plus extra for deep frying

4 large potatoes, chopped into long strips

3 large onions, finely chopped

3 large tomatoes, finely chopped

¼ tsp turmeric

1 tsp chilli powder

2 tsp ground coriander

1 tsp ground cumin

25 cashew nuts, coarsely crushed

4 kidneys, diced

500g/1lb 2oz lamb, chopped into 5cm/2in pieces

Juice of 1 lemon

1 tsp ground black pepper

Salt to taste

500ml/16fl oz water

4 hard-boiled eggs, quartered

10g/¼oz coriander leaves, finely chopped

For the spice mixture:

1½ tsp ginger paste

1½ tsp garlic paste

4-5 green chillies

4 cardamom pods

6 cloves

1 tsp black cumin

1½ tbsp malt vinegar

Method

- Mix all the ingredients for the spice mixture together and grind with enough water to form a smooth paste. Set aside.
- Heat the oil for deep frying in a frying pan. Add the potatoes and deep fry on a medium heat for 3-4 minutes. Drain and set aside.
- Heat 5 tbsp oil in a saucepan. Add the onions and fry them on a medium heat till they turn translucent.
- Add the spice mixture paste. Fry for 2-3 minutes, stirring frequently.
- Add the tomatoes, turmeric, chilli powder, ground coriander and ground cumin. Continue to fry for 2-3 minutes.

- Add the cashew nuts, kidneys and the lamb. Fry for 6-7 minutes.
- Add the lemon juice, pepper, salt and water. Mix well. Cover with a lid and simmer for 45 minutes, stirring occasionally.
- Garnish with the eggs and coriander leaves. Serve hot.

Gosht Gulfaam

(Mutton with Goat's Cheese)

Serves 4

Ingredients

675g/1½lb boneless mutton

300g/10oz goat's cheese, drained

200g/7oz khoya*

150g/5½oz mixed dry fruit, finely chopped

6 green chillies, finely chopped

25g/scant 1 oz coriander leaves, finely chopped

2 hard-boiled eggs

For the sauce:

¾ tbsp refined vegetable oil

3 large onions, finely chopped

5cm/2in root ginger, finely chopped

10 garlic cloves, finely chopped

3 tomatoes, finely chopped

1 tsp chilli powder

120ml/4fl oz lamb stock

Salt to taste

Method
- Pat the mutton flat till it resembles a steak.
- Mix the goat's cheese, khoya, dry fruits, green chillies and coriander leaves together. Knead this mixture to a soft dough.
- Spread the dough out over the flattened mutton and place the eggs in the centre.
- Roll the mutton tightly so that the dough and eggs remain inside. Wrap in foil and bake in an oven at 180°C (350°F, Gas Mark 4) for 1 hour. Set aside.
- To prepare the sauce, heat the oil in a saucepan. Add the onions and fry on a medium heat till they turn translucent.
- Add the ginger and garlic. Fry for a minute.
- Add the tomatoes and chilli powder. Continue to fry for 2 minutes, stirring frequently.
- Add the stock and salt. Mix well. Simmer for 10 minutes, stirring occasionally. Set aside.
- Slice the baked meat roll and arrange the slices in a serving dish. Pour the sauce over them and serve hot.

Lamb Do Pyaaza

(Lamb with Onions)

Serves 4

Ingredients

120ml/4fl oz refined vegetable oil

1 tsp turmeric

3 bay leaves

4 cloves

5cm/2in cinnamon

6 dry red chillies

4 green cardamom pods

6 large onions, 2 chopped, 4 sliced

3 tbsp ginger paste

3 tbsp garlic paste

2 tomatoes, finely chopped

8 shallots, halved

2 tsp garam masala

2 tsp ground coriander

4 tsp ground cumin

1½ tsp grated mace

½ grated nutmeg

2 tsp ground black pepper

Salt to taste

675g/1½lb lamb, diced

250ml/8fl oz water

10g/¼oz coriander leaves, finely chopped

2.5cm/1in root ginger, julienned

Method

- Heat the oil in a saucepan. Add the turmeric, bay leaves, cloves, cinnamon, red chillies and cardamom. Let them splutter for 30 seconds.
- Add the chopped onions. Fry them on a medium heat till they turn translucent.
- Add the ginger paste and garlic paste. Fry for a minute.
- Add the tomatoes, shallots, garam masala, ground coriander, ground cumin, mace, nutmeg, pepper and salt. Continue to fry for 2-3 minutes.
- Add the lamb and the sliced onions. Mix well and fry for 6-7 minutes.
- Add the water and stir for a minute. Cover with a lid and simmer for 30 minutes, stirring occasionally.
- Garnish with the coriander leaves and the ginger. Serve hot.

Fish Kebab

Serves 4

Ingredients

1kg/2¼lb swordfish, skinned and filleted

4 tbsp refined vegetable oil plus extra for frying

75g/2½oz chana dhal*, soaked in 250ml/9oz water for 30 minutes

3 cloves

½ tsp cumin seeds

2.5cm/1in root ginger, grated

10 garlic cloves

2.5cm/1in cinnamon

2 black cardamom pods

8 black peppercorns

4 dry red chillies

¾ tsp turmeric

1 tbsp Greek yoghurt

1 tsp black cumin seeds

For the stuffing:

2 dry figs, finely chopped

4 dry apricots, finely chopped

Juice of 1 lemon

10g/¼oz mint leaves, finely chopped

10g/¼oz coriander leaves, finely chopped

Salt to taste

Method

- Steam the fish in a steamer on a medium heat for 10 minutes. Set aside.

- Heat 2 tbsp oil in a frying pan. Drain the dhal and fry it on a medium heat till it turns golden brown.

- Mix the dhal with the cloves, cumin seeds, ginger, garlic, cinnamon, cardamom, peppercorns, red chillies, turmeric, yoghurt and black cumin seeds. Grind this mixture with enough water to form a smooth paste. Set aside.

- Heat 2 tbsp oil in a saucepan. Add this paste and fry it on a medium heat for 4-5 minutes.

- Add the steamed fish. Mix thoroughly and stir for 2 minutes.

- Divide the mixture into 8 portions and shape into patties. Set aside.

- Mix all the stuffing ingredients together. Divide into 8 portions.

- Flatten the patties and carefully place a portion of the stuffing on each patty. Seal like a pouch and roll again to form a ball. Pat the balls flat.

- Heat the oil for frying in a frying pan. Add the patties and shallow fry them on a medium heat till they turn golden brown. Flip and repeat.

- Drain on absorbent paper and serve hot.

Fish Chops

Serves 4

Ingredients

500g/1lb 2oz monkfish tail, skinned and filleted

500ml/16fl oz water

Salt to taste

1 tbsp refined vegetable oil plus extra for deep frying

1 tbsp ginger paste

1 tbsp garlic paste

1 large onion, finely grated

4 green chillies, grated

½ tsp turmeric

1 tsp garam masala

1 tsp ground cumin

1 tsp chilli powder

1 tomato, blanched and sliced

25g/scant 1oz coriander leaves, finely chopped

2 tbsp mint leaves, finely chopped

400g/14oz cooked peas

2 bread slices, soaked in water and drained

50g/1¾oz breadcrumbs

Method

- Place the fish with the water in a saucepan. Add the salt and boil on a medium heat for 20 minutes. Drain and set aside.

- For the filling, heat 1 tbsp of the oil in a saucepan. Add the ginger paste, garlic paste and onion. Sauté on a medium heat for 2-3 minutes.

- Add the green chillies, turmeric, garam masala, ground cumin and chilli powder. Fry for a minute.

- Add the tomato. Fry for 3-4 minutes.

- Add the coriander leaves, mint leaves, peas and bread slices. Mix well. Cook on a low heat for 7-8 minutes, stirring occasionally. Remove from the heat and knead the mixture well. Divide into 8 equal-sized portions and set aside.

- Mash the boiled fish and divide into 8 portions.

- Shape each fish portion like a cup and stuff it with a portion of the filling mixture. Seal like a pouch, roll into a ball and shape like a cutlet. Repeat for the remainng fish portions and the filling mixture.

- Heat the oil for deep frying in a pan. Roll the cutlets in the breadcrumbs and deep fry them on a medium heat till they turn golden brown. Serve hot.

Fish Sookha

(Dry Fish in Spices)

Serves 4

Ingredients

1cm/½in root ginger

10 garlic cloves

1 tbsp coriander leaves, finely chopped

3 green chillies

1 tsp turmeric

3 tsp chilli powder

Salt to taste

1kg/2¼lb swordfish, skinned and filleted

50g/1¾oz desiccated coconut

6-7 kokum*, soaked for 1 hour in 120ml/4fl oz water

4 tbsp refined vegetable oil

60ml/2fl oz water

Method

- Mix the ginger, garlic, coriander leaves, green chillies, turmeric, chilli powder and salt together. Grind this mixture to a smooth paste.

- Marinate the fish with the paste for 1 hour.

- Heat a saucepan. Add the coconut. Dry roast on a medium heat for a minute.

- Discard the kokum berries and add the kokum water. Mix well. Remove from the heat and add this mixture to the marinated fish.

- Heat the oil in a saucepan. Add the fish mixture and cook on a medium heat for 4-5 minutes.

- Add the water. Mix well. Cover with a lid and simmer for 20 minutes, stirring occasionally.

- Serve hot.

Mahya Kalia

(Fish with Coconut, Sesame Seeds and Peanuts)

Serves 4

Ingredients

100g/3½oz fresh coconut, grated

1 tsp sesame seeds

1 tbsp peanuts

1 tbsp tamarind paste

1 tsp turmeric

1 tsp ground coriander

Salt to taste

250ml/8fl oz water

500g/1lb 2oz swordfish fillets

1 tbsp coriander leaves, chopped

Method

- Dry roast the coconut, sesame seeds and peanuts together. Mix with the tamarind paste, turmeric, ground coriander and salt. Grind with enough water to form a smooth paste.

- Cook this mixture with the remaining water in a saucepan on a medium heat for 10 minutes, stirring frequently. Add the fish fillets and simmer for 10-12 minutes. Garnish with the coriander leaves and serve hot.

Prawn Curry Rosachi

(Prawns cooked with Coconut)

Serves 4

Ingredients

200g/7oz fresh coconut, grated

5 red chillies

1½ tsp coriander seeds

1½ tsp poppy seeds

1 tsp cumin seeds

½ tsp turmeric

6 garlic cloves

120ml/4fl oz refined vegetable oil

2 large onions, finely chopped

2 tomatoes, finely chopped

250g/9oz prawns, shelled and de-veined

Salt to taste

Method

- Grind the coconut, red chillies, coriander, poppy seeds, cumin seeds, turmeric and garlic with enough water to form a smooth paste. Set aside.

- Heat the oil in a saucepan. Fry the onions on a low heat till brown.

- Add the ground coconut-red chillies paste, tomatoes, prawns and salt. Mix well. Cook for 15 minutes, stirring occasionally. Serve hot.

Fish Stuffed with Dates & Almonds

Serves 4

Ingredients

4 trout, 250g/9oz each, slit vertically

½ tsp chilli powder

1 tsp ginger paste

250g/9oz fresh seedless dates, blanched and finely chopped

75g/2½oz almonds, blanched and finely chopped

2-3 tbsp steamed rice (see here)

1 tsp sugar

¼ tsp ground cinnamon

½ tsp ground black pepper

Salt to taste

1 large onion, finely sliced

Method

- Marinate the fish with the chilli powder and ginger paste for 1 hour.

- Mix the dates, almonds, rice, sugar, cinnamon, pepper and salt together. Knead to form a soft dough. Set aside.

- Stuff the date-almond dough in the slits of the marinated fish. Place the stuffed fish on a sheet of aluminium foil and sprinkle the onion on top.

- Wrap the fish and onion inside the foil and seal the edges firmly.

- Bake in an oven at 200°C (400°F, Gas Mark 6) for 15-20 minutes. Unwrap the foil and bake the fish for 5 more minutes. Serve hot.

Tandoori Fish

Serves 4

Ingredients

1 tsp ginger paste

1 tsp garlic paste

½ tsp garam masala

1 tsp chilli powder

1 tbsp lemon juice

Salt to taste

500g/1lb 2oz monkfish tail fillets

1 tbsp chaat masala*

Method

- Mix together the ginger paste, garlic paste, garam masala, chilli powder, lemon juice and salt.

- Make incisions on the fish. Marinate with the ginger-garlic mixture for 2 hours.

- Grill the fish for 15 minutes. Sprinkle with the chaat masala. Serve hot.

Fish with Vegetables

Serves 4

Ingredients

750g/1lb 10oz salmon fillets, skinned

½ tsp turmeric

Salt to taste

2 tbsp mustard oil

¼ tsp mustard seeds

¼ tsp fennel seeds

¼ tsp onion seeds

¼ tsp fenugreek seeds

¼ tsp cumin seeds

2 bay leaves

2 dry red chillies, halved

1 large onion, finely sliced

2 large green chillies, slit lengthways

½ tsp sugar

125g/4½oz canned peas

1 large potato, chopped into strips

2-3 small aubergines, julienned

250ml/8fl oz water

Method

- Marinate the fish with the turmeric and salt for 30 minutes.

- Heat the oil in a saucepan. Add the marinated fish and fry on a medium heat for 4-5 minutes, turning occasionally. Drain and set aside.

- To the same oil, add the mustard, fennel, onion, fenugreek and cumin seeds. Let them splutter for 15 seconds.

- Add the bay leaves and red chillies. Fry for 30 seconds.

- Add the onion and green chillies. Fry on a medium heat till the onion turns brown.

- Add the sugar, peas, potato and aubergines. Mix well. Stir-fry the mixture for 7-8 minutes.

- Add the fried fish and the water. Mix well. Cover with a lid and simmer for 12-15 minutes, stirring occasionally.

- Serve hot.

Tandoor Gulnar

(Trout cooked in a Tandoor)

Serves 4

Ingredients

4 trout, 250g/9oz each

Butter for basting

For the first marinade:

120ml/4fl oz malt vinegar

2 tbsp lemon juice

2 tsp garlic paste

½ tsp chilli powder

Salt to taste

For the second marinade:

400g/14oz yoghurt

1 egg

1 tsp garlic paste

2 tsp ginger paste

120ml/4fl oz fresh single cream

180g/6½oz besan*

Prawns in Green Masala

Serves 4

Ingredients

1cm/½in root ginger

8 garlic cloves

3 green chillies, slit lengthways

50g/1¾oz coriander leaves, chopped

1½ tbsp refined vegetable oil

2 large onions, finely chopped

2 tomatoes, finely chopped

500g/1lb 2oz large prawns, shelled and de-veined

1 tsp tamarind paste

Salt to taste

½ tsp turmeric

Method

- Grind together the ginger, garlic, chillies and coriander leaves. Set aside.
- Heat the oil in a saucepan. Fry the onions on a low heat till brown.
- Add the ginger-garlic paste and the tomatoes. Fry for 4-5 minutes.
- Add the prawns, tamarind paste, salt and turmeric. Mix well. Cook for 15 minutes, stirring occasionally. Serve hot.

Fish Cutlet

Serves 4

Ingredients

2 eggs

1 tbsp plain white flour

Salt to taste

400g/14oz John Dory, skinned and filleted

500ml/16fl oz water

2 large potatoes, boiled and mashed

1½ tsp garam masala

1 large onion, grated

1 tsp ginger paste

Refined vegetable oil for deep frying

200g/7oz breadcrumbs

Method

- Whisk the eggs with the flour and salt. Set aside.
- Cook the fish in salted water in a saucepan on a medium heat for 15-20 minutes. Drain and knead with the potatoes, garam masala, onion, ginger paste and salt to a soft dough.
- Divide into 16 portions, roll into balls and flatten lightly to form cutlets.
- Heat the oil in a pan. Dip the cutlets in the whisked egg, roll in the breadcrumbs and deep fry on a low heat till golden brown. Serve hot.

Parsi Fish Sas

(Fish cooked in White Sauce)

Serves 4

Ingredients

1 tbsp rice flour

1 tbsp sugar

60ml/2fl oz malt vinegar

2 tbsp refined vegetable oil

2 large onions, finely sliced

½ tsp ginger paste

½ tsp garlic paste

1 tsp ground cumin

Salt to taste

250ml/8fl oz water

8 fillets lemon sole

2 eggs, whisked

Method

- Grind the rice flour with the sugar and vinegar to a paste. Set aside.
- Heat the oil in a saucepan. Fry the onions on a low heat till brown.
- Add the ginger paste, garlic paste, ground cumin, salt, water and fish. Cook on a low heat for 25 minutes, stirring occasionally.
- Add the flour mixture and cook for a minute.
- Gently add the eggs. Stir for a minute. Garnish and serve hot.

Peshawari Machhi

Serves 4

Ingredients

3 tbsp refined vegetable oil

1kg/2¼lb salmon, sliced into steaks

2.5cm/1in root ginger, grated

8 garlic cloves, crushed

2 large onions, ground

3 tomatoes, blanched and chopped

1 tsp garam masala

400g/14oz yoghurt

¾ tsp turmeric

1 tsp amchoor*

Salt to taste

Method

- Heat the oil. Fry the fish on a low heat till golden. Drain and set aside.
- To the same oil, add the ginger, garlic and onions. Fry on a low heat for 6 minutes. Add the fried fish and all the remaining ingredients. Mix well.
- Simmer for 20 minutes and serve hot.

Crab Curry

Serves 4

Ingredients

4 medium-sized crabs, cleaned (see <u>cooking techniques</u>)

Salt to taste

1 tsp turmeric

½ coconut, grated

6 garlic cloves

4-5 red chillies

1 tbsp coriander seeds

1 tbsp cumin seeds

1 tsp tamarind paste

3-4 green chillies, slit lengthways

1 tbsp refined vegetable oil

1 large onion, finely chopped

Method

- Marinate the crabs with the salt and turmeric for 30 minutes.
- Grind all the remaining ingredients, except the oil and onion, with enough water to form a smooth paste.
- Heat the oil in a saucepan. Fry the ground paste and the onion on a low heat till the onion are brown. Add some water. Simmer for 7-8 minutes, stirring occasionally. Add the marinated crabs. Mix well and simmer for 5 minutes. Serve hot.

Mustard Fish

Serves 4

Ingredients

8 tbsp mustard oil

4 trout, 250g/9oz each

2 tsp ground cumin

2 tsp ground mustard

1 tsp ground coriander

½ tsp turmeric

120ml/4fl oz water

Salt to taste

Method

- Heat the oil in a saucepan. Add the fish and fry it on a medium heat for 1-2 minutes. Flip the fish and repeat. Drain and set aside.
- To the same oil, add the ground cumin, mustard and coriander. Let them splutter for 15 seconds.
- Add the turmeric, water, salt and the fried fish. Mix well and simmer for 10-12 minutes. Serve hot.

Meen Vattichathu

(Red Fish cooked with Spices)

Serves 4

Ingredients

600g/1lb 5oz swordfish, skinned and filleted

½ tsp turmeric

Salt to taste

3 tbsp refined vegetable oil

½ tsp mustard seeds

½ tsp fenugreek seeds

8 curry leaves

2 large onions, finely sliced

8 garlic cloves, finely chopped

5cm/2in ginger, finely sliced

6 kokum*

Method

- Marinate the fish with the turmeric and salt for 2 hours.
- Heat the oil in a saucepan. Add the mustard and fenugreek seeds. Let them splutter for 15 seconds. Add all the remaining ingredients and the marinated fish. Stir-fry on a low heat for 15 minutes. Serve hot.

Doi Maach

(Fish cooked in Yoghurt)

Serves 4

Ingredients

4 trout, skinned and filleted

2 tbsp refined vegetable oil

2 bay leaves

1 large onion, finely chopped

2 tsp sugar

Salt to taste

200g/7oz yoghurt

For the marinade:

3 cloves

5cm/2in piece cinnamon

3 green cardamom pods

5cm/2in root ginger

1 large onion, finely sliced

1 tsp turmeric

Salt to taste

Method

- Grind all the marinade ingredients together. Marinate the fish with this mixture for 30 minutes.
- Heat the oil in a saucepan. Add the bay leaves and onion. Fry on a low heat for 3 minutes. Add the sugar, salt and the marinated fish. Mix well.
- Sauté for 10 minutes. Add the yoghurt and cook for 8 minutes. Serve hot.

Fish Fry

Serves 4

Ingredients

6 tbsp besan*

2 tsp garam masala

1 tsp amchoor*

1 tsp ajowan seeds

1 tsp ginger paste

1 tsp garlic paste

Salt to taste

675g/1½lb monkfish tail, skinned and filleted

Refined vegetable oil for deep frying

Method

- Mix together all the ingredients, except the fish and the oil, with enough water to form a thick batter. Marinate the fish with this batter for 4 hours.
- Heat the oil in a frying pan. Add the fish and deep fry on a medium heat for 4-5 minutes. Flip and fry again for 2-3 minutes. Serve hot.

Machher Chop

Serves 4

Ingredients

500g/1lb 2oz salmon, skinned and filleted

Salt to taste

500ml/16fl oz water

250g/9oz potatoes, boiled and mashed

200ml/7fl oz mustard oil

2 large onions, finely chopped

½ tsp ginger paste

½ tsp garlic paste

1½ tsp garam masala

1 egg, whisked

200g/7oz breadcrumbs

Refined vegetable oil for deep frying

Method

- Place the fish with the salt and water in a saucepan. Cook on a medium heat for 15 minutes. Drain and mash with the potatoes. Set aside.
- Heat the oil in a frying pan. Add the onions and fry on a medium heat till brown. Add the fish mixture and all

the remaining ingredients, except the egg and breadcrumbs. Mix well and cook on a low heat for 10 minutes.
- Cool and divide into lemon-sized balls. Flatten and shape into cutlets.
- Heat the oil for deep frying in a pan. Dip the cutlets in the egg, roll in the breadcrumbs and deep fry on a medium heat till golden. Serve hot.

Goa Swordfish

(Swordfish cooked in Goan Style)

Serves 4

Ingredients

50g/1¾oz fresh coconut, grated

1 tsp coriander seeds

1 tsp cumin seeds

1 tsp poppy seeds

4 garlic cloves

1 tbsp tamarind paste

250ml/8fl oz water

Refined vegetable oil for frying

1 large onion, finely chopped

1 tbsp kokum*

Salt to taste

½ tsp turmeric

4 swordfish steaks

Method

- Grind together the coconut, coriander seeds, cumin seeds, poppy seeds, garlic and tamarind paste with enough water to form a smooth paste. Set aside.
- Heat the oil in a saucepan. Add the onion and fry it on a medium heat till it turns brown.
- Add the ground paste and fry for 2 minutes. Add the remaining ingredients. Mix well and simmer for 15 minutes. Serve hot.

Dry Fish Masala

Serves 4

Ingredients

6 salmon fillets

¼ fresh coconut, grated

7 red chillies

1 tbsp turmeric

Salt to taste

Method

- Grill the fish fillets for 20 minutes. Set aside.
- Grind together the remaining ingredients to form a smooth paste.
- Mix with the fish. Cook the mixture in a saucepan on a low heat for 15 minutes. Serve hot.

Madras Prawn Curry

Serves 4

Ingredients

3 tbsp refined vegetable oil

3 large onions, finely chopped

12 garlic cloves, minced

3 tomatoes, blanched and chopped

½ tsp turmeric

Salt to taste

1 tsp chilli powder

2 tbsp tamarind paste

750g/1lb 10oz medium-sized prawns, shelled and de-veined

4 tbsp coconut milk

Method

- Heat the oil in a saucepan. Add the onions and garlic and fry on a medium heat for a minute. Add the tomatoes, turmeric, salt, chilli powder, tamarind paste and prawns. Mix well and fry for 7-8 minutes.
- Add the coconut milk. Simmer for 10 minutes and serve hot.

Fish in Fenugreek

Serves 4

Ingredients

8 tbsp refined vegetable oil

500g/1lb 2oz salmon, filleted

1 tbsp garlic paste

75g/2½oz fresh fenugreek leaves, finely chopped

4 tomatoes, finely chopped

2 tsp ground coriander

1 tsp ground cumin

1 tsp lemon juice

Salt to taste

1 tsp turmeric

75g/2½oz hot water

Method

- Heat 4 tbsp oil in a frying pan. Add the fish and shallow fry on a medium heat till golden brown on both sides. Drain and set aside.
- Heat 4 tbsp oil in a saucepan. Add the garlic paste. Fry on a low heat for a minute. Add the remaining ingredients, except the water. Stir-fry for 4-5 minutes.
- Add the water and the fried fish. Mix well. Cover with a lid and simmer for 10-15 minutes, stirring occasionally. Serve hot.

Karimeen Porichathu

(Fish Fillet in Masala)

Serves 4

Ingredients

1 tsp chilli powder

1 tbsp ground coriander

1 tsp turmeric

1 tsp ginger paste

2 green chillies, finely chopped

Juice of 1 lemon

8 curry leaves

Salt to taste

8 salmon fillets

Refined vegetable oil for frying

Method
- Mix together all the ingredients, except the fish and oil.
- Marinate the fish with this mixture and refrigerate for 2 hours.
- Heat the oil in a frying pan. Add the fish pieces and shallow fry them on a medium heat till golden brown.
- Serve hot.

Jumbo Prawns

Serves 4

Ingredients

500g/1lb 2oz large prawns, shelled and de-veined

1 tsp turmeric

½ tsp chilli powder

Salt to taste

3 tbsp refined vegetable oil

1 large onion, finely chopped

1cm/½in root ginger, finely chopped

10 garlic cloves, finely chopped

2-3 green chillies, slit lengthways

½ tsp sugar

250ml/8fl oz coconut milk

1 tbsp coriander leaves, finely chopped

Method

- Marinate the prawns with the turmeric, chilli powder and salt for 1 hour.
- Heat the oil in a saucepan. Add the onion, ginger, garlic and green chillies and fry on a medium heat for 2-3 minutes.
- Add the sugar, salt and the marinated prawns. Mix well and sauté for 10 minutes. Add the coconut milk. Simmer for 15 minutes.
- Garnish with the coriander leaves and serve hot.

Pickled Fish

Serves 4

Ingredients

Refined vegetable oil for frying

1kg/2¼lb swordfish, skinned and filleted

1 tsp turmeric

12 dry red chillies

1 tbsp cumin seeds

5cm/2in root ginger

15 garlic cloves

250ml/8fl oz malt vinegar

Salt to taste

Method

- Heat the oil in a frying pan. Add the fish and shallow fry on a medium heat for 2-3 minutes. Flip and fry for 1-2 minutes. Set aside.
- Grind the remaining ingredients together to form a smooth paste.
- Cook the paste in a pan on a low heat for 10 minutes. Add the fish, cook for 3-4 minutes, then cool and store in a jar, refrigerated, for up to 1 week.

Fish Ball Curry

Serves 4

Ingredients

500g/1lb 2oz salmon, skinned and filleted

Salt to taste

750ml/1¼ pints water

1 large onion

3 tsp garam masala

½ tsp turmeric

3 tbsp refined vegetable oil plus extra for deep frying

5cm/2in root ginger, grated

5 garlic cloves, crushed

250g/9oz tomatoes, blanched and diced

2 tbsp yoghurt, whisked

Method

- Cook the fish with some salt and 500ml/16fl oz water on a medium heat for 20 minutes. Drain and grind with the onion, salt, 1 tsp garam masala and the turmeric to a smooth mixture. Divide into 12 balls.
- Heat the oil for deep frying. Add the balls and deep fry on a medium heat till golden brown. Drain and set aside.
- Heat 3 tbsp oil in a saucepan. Add all the remaining ingredients, the remaining water and the fish balls. Simmer for 10 minutes and serve hot.

Fish Amritsari

(Hot Spicy Fish)

Serves 4

Ingredients

200g/7oz yoghurt

½ tsp ginger paste

½ tsp garlic paste

Juice of 1 lemon

½ tsp garam masala

Salt to taste

675g/1½lb monkfish tail, skinned and filleted

Method

- Mix together all the ingredients, except the fish. Marinate the fish with this mixture for 1 hour.
- Grill the marinated fish for 7-8 minutes. Serve hot.

Masala Fried Prawns

Serves 4

Ingredients

4 garlic cloves

5cm/2in ginger

2 tbsp fresh coconut, grated

2 dry red chillies

1 tbsp coriander seeds

1 tsp turmeric

Salt to taste

120ml/4fl oz water

750g/1lb 10oz prawns, shelled and de-veined

3 tbsp refined vegetable oil

3 large onions, finely chopped

2 tomatoes, finely chopped

2 tbsp coriander leaves, chopped

1 tsp garam masala

Method

- Grind together the garlic, ginger, coconut, red chillies, coriander seeds, turmeric and salt with enough water to form a smooth paste.
- Marinate the prawns with this paste for an hour.
- Heat the oil in a saucepan. Add the onions and fry them on a medium heat till translucent.
- Add the tomatoes and the marinated prawns. Mix well. Add the water, cover with a lid and simmer for 20 minutes.
- Garnish with the coriander leaves and garam masala. Serve hot.

Savoury Topped Fish

Serves 4

Ingredients

2 tbsp lemon juice

Salt to taste

Ground black pepper to taste

4 swordfish steaks

2 tbsp butter

1 large onion, finely chopped

1 green pepper, cored and chopped

3 tomatoes, skinned and chopped

50g/1¾oz breadcrumbs

85g/3oz Cheddar cheese, grated

Method

- Sprinkle the lemon juice, salt and pepper on top of the fish. Set aside.
- Heat the butter in a saucepan. Add the onion and green pepper. Fry on a medium heat for 2-3 minutes. Add the tomatoes, breadcrumbs and cheese. Fry for 4-5 minutes.
- Spread this mixture evenly over the fish. Wrap in aluminium foil and bake in an oven at 200°C (400°F, Gas Mark 6) for 30 minutes. Serve hot.

Prawn Pasanda

(Prawn cooked with Yoghurt and Vinegar)

Serves 4

Ingredients

250g/9oz prawns, shelled and de-veined

Salt to taste

1 tsp ground black pepper

2 tsp malt vinegar

2 tsp refined vegetable oil

1 tbsp garlic paste

2 large onions, finely chopped

2 tomatoes, finely chopped

2 spring onions, finely chopped

1 tsp garam masala

250ml/8fl oz water

4 tbsp Greek yoghurt

Method

- Marinate the prawns with the salt, pepper and vinegar for 30 minutes.
- Grill the prawns for 5 minutes. Set aside.
- Heat the oil in a saucepan. Add the garlic paste and onions. Fry on a medium heat for a minute. Add the tomatoes, spring onions and garam masala. Sauté for 4 minutes. Add the grilled prawns and water. Cook on a low heat for 15 minutes. Add the yoghurt. Stir for 5 minutes. Serve hot.

Swordfish Rechaido

(Swordfish cooked in Goan Gravy)

Serves 4

Ingredients

4 red chillies

6 garlic cloves

2.5cm/1in root ginger

½ tsp turmeric

1 large onion

1 tsp tamarind paste

1 tsp cumin seeds

1 tbsp sugar

Salt to taste

120ml/4fl oz malt vinegar

1kg/2¼lb swordfish, cleaned

Refined vegetable oil for frying

Method

- Grind together all the ingredients, except the fish and oil.
- Make slits on the swordfish and marinate with the ground mixture, stuffing ample amounts of the mixture in the slits. Set aside for 1 hour.
- Heat the oil in a frying pan. Add the marinated fish and shallow fry on a low heat for 2-3 minutes. Flip and repeat. Serve hot.

Teekha Jhinga

(Hot Prawns)

Serves 4

Ingredients

4 tbsp refined vegetable oil

1 tsp fennel seeds

2 large onions, finely chopped

2 tsp ginger paste

2 tsp garlic paste

Salt to taste

½ tsp turmeric

3 tbsp garam masala

25g/scant 1oz desiccated coconut

60ml/2fl oz water

1 tbsp lemon juice

500g/1lb 2oz prawns, shelled and de-veined

Method

- Heat the oil in a saucepan. Add the fennel seeds. Let them splutter for 15 seconds. Add the onions, ginger paste and garlic paste. Fry on a medium heat for a minute.
- Add the remaining ingredients, except the prawns. Sauté for 7 minutes.
- Add the prawns and cook for 15 minutes, stirring frequently. Serve hot.

Prawns Balchow

(Prawns cooked the Goan Way)

Serves 4

Ingredients

750g/1lb 10oz prawns, shelled and de-veined

250ml/8fl oz malt vinegar

8 garlic cloves

2 large onions, finely chopped

1 tbsp ground cumin

¼ tsp turmeric

Salt to taste

120ml/4fl oz refined vegetable oil

50g/1¾oz coriander leaves, chopped

Method

- Marinate the prawns with 4 tbsp of the vinegar for 2 hours.
- Grind the remaining vinegar with the garlic, onions, ground cumin, turmeric and salt to form a smooth paste. Set aside.
- Heat the oil in a saucepan. Fry the prawns on a low heat for 12 minutes.

- Add the paste. Mix well and sauté on a low heat for 15 minutes.
- Garnish with the coriander leaves. Serve hot.

Prawns Bhujna

(Dry Prawns in Coconut and Onion)

Serves 4

Ingredients

50g/1¾oz fresh coconut, grated

2 large onions

6 red chillies

5cm/2in root ginger, grated

1 tsp garlic paste

4 tbsp refined vegetable oil

5 dry kokum*

¼ tsp turmeric

750g/1lb 10oz prawns, shelled and de-veined

250ml/8fl oz water

Salt to taste

Method

- Grind together the coconut, onions, red chillies, ginger and garlic paste.
- Heat the oil in a saucepan. Add the paste with the kokum and turmeric. Fry on a low heat for 5 minutes.
- Add the prawns, the water and salt. Simmer for 20 minutes, stirring frequently. Serve hot.

Chingdi Macher Malai

(Prawns in Coconut)

Serves 4

Ingredients

2 large onions, grated

2 tbsp ginger paste

100g/3½oz fresh coconut, grated

4 tbsp refined vegetable oil

500g/1lb 2oz prawns, shelled and de-veined

1 tsp turmeric

1 tsp ground cumin

4 tomatoes, finely chopped

1 tsp sugar

1 tsp ghee

2 cloves

2.5cm/1in cinnamon

2 green cardamom pods

3 bay leaves

Salt to taste

4 large potatoes, diced and fried

250ml/8fl oz water

Method

- Grind the onions, ginger paste and coconut to a smooth paste. Set aside.
- Heat the oil in a frying pan. Add the prawns and fry them on a medium heat for 5 minutes. Drain and set aside.
- To the same oil, add the ground paste and all the remaining ingredients, except the water. Stir-fry for 6-7 minutes. Add the fried prawns and the water. Mix well and simmer for 10 minutes. Serve hot.

Fish Sorse Bata

(Fish in Mustard Paste)

Serves 4

Ingredients

4 tbsp mustard seeds

7 green chillies

2 tbsp water

½ tsp turmeric

5 tbsp mustard oil

Salt to taste

1kg/2¼lb lemon sole, skinned and filleted

Method

- Grind together all the ingredients, except the fish, with enough water to form a smooth paste. Marinate the fish with this mixture for 1 hour.
- Steam for 25 minutes. Serve hot.

Fish Stew

Serves 4

Ingredients

1 tbsp refined vegetable oil

2 cloves

2.5cm/1in cinnamon

3 bay leaves

5 black peppercorns

1 tsp garlic paste

1 tsp ginger paste

2 large onions, finely chopped

400g/14oz frozen mixed vegetables

Salt to taste

250ml/8fl oz warm water

500g/1lb 2oz monkfish fillets

1 tbsp plain white flour, dissolved in 60ml/2fl oz milk

Method

- Heat the oil in a saucepan. Add the cloves, cinnamon, bay leaves and peppercorns. Let them splutter for 15 seconds. Add the garlic paste, ginger paste and onions. Fry on a medium heat for 2-3 minutes.
- Add the vegetables, salt and water. Mix well and simmer for 10 minutes.
- Carefully add the fish and the flour mixture. Mix well. Cook on a medium heat for 10 minutes. Serve hot.

Jhinga Nissa

(Prawns with Yoghurt)

Serves 4

Ingredients

1 tbsp lemon juice

1 tsp ginger paste

1 tsp garlic paste

1 tsp sesame seeds

200g/7oz yoghurt

2 green chillies, finely chopped

½ tsp dry fenugreek leaves

½ tsp ground cloves

½ tsp ground cinnamon

½ tsp ground black pepper

Salt to taste

12 large prawns, shelled and de-veined

Method

- Mix together all the ingredients, except the prawns. Marinate the prawns with this mixture for an hour.
- Arrange the marinated prawns on skewers and grill for 15 minutes. Serve hot.

Squid Vindaloo

(Squid cooked in Spicy Goan Gravy)

Serves 4

Ingredients

8 tbsp malt vinegar

8 red chillies

3.5cm/1½in root ginger

20 garlic cloves

1 tsp mustard seeds

1 tsp cumin seeds

1 tsp turmeric

Salt to taste

6 tbsp refined vegetable oil

3 large onions, finely chopped

500g/1lb 2oz squid, sliced

Method

- Grind half the vinegar with the red chillies, ginger, garlic, mustard seeds, cumin seeds, turmeric and salt to a smooth paste. Set aside.
- Heat the oil in a saucepan. Fry the onions on a low heat till brown.
- Add the ground paste. Mix well and sauté for 5-6 minutes.
- Add the squid and the remaining vinegar. Cook on a low heat for 15-20 minutes, stirring occasionally. Serve hot.

Lobster Balchow

(Spicy Lobsters cooked in Goan Curry)

Serves 4

Ingredients

400g/14oz lobster meat, chopped

Salt to taste

½ tsp turmeric

60ml/2fl oz malt vinegar

1 tsp sugar

120ml/4fl oz refined vegetable oil

2 large onions, finely chopped

12 garlic cloves, finely chopped

1 tsp garam masala

1 tbsp coriander leaves, chopped

Method

- Marinate the lobster with the salt, turmeric, vinegar and sugar for 1 hour.
- Heat the oil in a saucepan. Add the onions and garlic. Fry on a low heat for 2-3 minutes. Add the marinated lobster and the garam masala. Cook on a low heat for 15 minutes, stirring occasionally.
- Garnish with the coriander leaves. Serve hot.

Prawns with Aubergine

Serves 4

Ingredients

4 tbsp refined vegetable oil

6 black peppercorns

3 green chillies

4 cloves

6 garlic cloves

1cm/½in root ginger

2 tbsp coriander leaves, chopped

1½ tbsp desiccated coconut

2 large onions, finely chopped

500g/1lb 2oz aubergines, chopped

250g/9oz prawns, shelled and de-veined

½ tsp turmeric

1 tsp tamarind paste

Salt to taste

10 cashew nuts

120ml/4fl oz water

Method

- Heat 1 tbsp of the oil in a saucepan. Add the peppercorns, green chillies, cloves, garlic, ginger, coriander leaves and coconut on a medium heat for 2-3 minutes. Grind the mixture to a smooth paste. Set aside.
- Heat the remaining oil in a saucepan. Add the onions and fry on a medium heat for a minute. Add the aubergines, prawns and turmeric. Stir-fry for 5 minutes.
- Add the ground paste and all the remaining ingredients. Mix well and simmer for 10-15 minutes. Serve hot.

Green Prawns

Serves 4

Ingredients

Juice of 1 lemon

50g/1¾oz mint leaves

50g/1¾oz coriander leaves

4 green chillies

2.5cm/1in root ginger

8 garlic cloves

Pinch of garam masala

Salt to taste

20 medium-sized prawns, shelled and de-veined

Method

- Grind together all the ingredients, except the prawns, to a smooth paste. Marinate the prawns with this mixture for 1 hour.
- Skewer the prawns. Grill for 10 minutes, turning occasionally. Serve hot.

Fish with Coriander

Serves 4

Ingredients

3 tbsp refined vegetable oil

1 large onion, finely chopped

4 green chillies, finely chopped

1 tbsp ginger paste

1 tbsp garlic paste

1 tsp turmeric

Salt to taste

100g/3½oz coriander leaves, chopped

1kg/2¼lb salmon, skinned and filleted

250ml/8fl oz water

Method

- Heat the oil in a saucepan. Fry the onion on a low heat till brown.
- Add all the remaining ingredients, except the fish and water. Fry for 3-4 minutes. Add the fish and sauté for 3-4 minutes.
- Add the water. Mix well and simmer for 10-12 minutes. Serve hot.

Fish Malai

(Fish cooked in Creamy Gravy)

Serves 4

Ingredients

250ml/8fl oz refined vegetable oil

1kg/2¼lb sea bass fillets

1 tbsp plain white flour

1 large onion, grated

½ tsp turmeric

250ml/8fl oz coconut milk

Salt to taste

For the spice mixture:

1 tsp coriander seeds

1 tsp cumin seeds

4 green chillies

6 garlic cloves

6 tbsp water

Method

- Grind the spice mixture ingredients together. Squeeze the mixture to extract its juice in a small bowl. Set the juice aside. Discard the husk.
- Heat the oil in a frying pan. Coat the fish with the flour and deep fry on a medium heat till golden brown. Drain and set aside.
- To the same oil, add the onion and fry on a medium heat till brown.
- Add the spice mixture juice and all the remaining ingredients. Mix well.
- Simmer for 10 minutes. Add the fish and cook for 5 minutes. Serve hot.

Konkani Fish Curry

Serves 4

Ingredients

1kg/2¼lb salmon, skinned and filleted

Salt to taste

1 tsp turmeric

1 tsp chilli powder

2 tbsp refined vegetable oil

1 large onion, finely chopped

½ tsp ginger paste

750ml/1¼ pints coconut milk

3 green chillies, slit lengthways

Method

- Marinate the fish with the salt, turmeric and chilli powder for 30 minutes.
- Heat the oil in a saucepan. Add the onion and ginger paste. Fry on a medium heat till the onions turn translucent.
- Add the coconut milk, green chillies and the marinated fish. Mix well. Simmer for 15 minutes. Serve hot.

Spicy Prawns with Garlic

Serves 4

Ingredients

4 tbsp refined vegetable oil

2 large onions, finely chopped

1 tbsp garlic paste

12 garlic cloves, chopped

1 tsp chilli powder

1 tsp ground coriander

½ tsp ground cumin

2 tomatoes, finely chopped

Salt to taste

1 tsp turmeric

750g/1lb 10oz prawns, shelled and de-veined

250ml/8fl oz water

Method

- Heat the oil in a saucepan. Add the onions, garlic paste and chopped garlic. Fry on a medium heat till the onions turn translucent.
- Add the remaining ingredients, except the prawns and water. Fry for 3-4 minutes. Add the prawns and sauté for 3-4 minutes.
- Add the water. Mix well and simmer for 12-15 minutes. Serve hot.

Simple Fish Curry

Serves 4

Ingredients

2 large onions, quartered

3 cloves

2.5cm/1in cinnamon

4 black peppercorns

2 tsp coriander seeds

1 tsp cumin seeds

1 tomato, quartered

Salt to taste

2 tbsp refined vegetable oil

750g/1lb 10oz salmon, skinned and filleted

250ml/8fl oz water

Method

- Grind together all the ingredients, except the oil, fish and water. Heat the oil in a saucepan. Add the paste and fry on a low heat for 7 minutes.
- Add the fish and water. Cook for 25 minutes, stirring frequently. Serve hot.

Goan Fish Curry

Serves 4

Ingredients

100g/3½oz fresh coconut, grated

4 dry red chillies

1 tsp cumin seeds

1 tsp coriander seeds

360ml/12fl oz water

3 tbsp refined vegetable oil

1 large onion, grated

1 tsp turmeric

8 curry leaves

2 tomatoes, blanched and chopped

2 green chillies, slit lengthways

1 tbsp tamarind paste

Salt to taste

1kg/2¼lb salmon, sliced

Method

- Grind the coconut, red chillies, cumin seeds and coriander seeds with 4 tbsp water into a thick paste. Set aside.
- Heat the oil in a saucepan. Fry the onion on a low heat till translucent.
- Add the coconut paste. Fry for 3-4 minutes.
- Add all the remaining ingredients, except the fish and remaining water. Sauté for 6-7 minutes. Add the fish and water. Mix well and simmer for 20 minutes, stirring occasionally. Serve hot.

Prawn Vindaloo

(Prawns cooked in Spicy Goan Curry)

Serves 4

Ingredients

- 3 tbsp refined vegetable oil
- 1 large onion, grated
- 4 tomatoes, finely chopped
- 1½ tsp chilli powder
- ½ tsp turmeric
- 2 tsp ground cumin
- 750g/1lb 10oz prawns, shelled and de-veined
- 3 tbsp white vinegar
- 1 tsp sugar
- Salt to taste

Method

- Heat the oil in a saucepan. Add the onion and fry on a medium heat for 1-2 minutes. Add the tomatoes, chilli powder, turmeric and cumin. Mix well and cook for 6-7 minutes, stirring occasionally.
- Add the prawns and mix well. Cook on a low heat for 10 minutes.
- Add the vinegar, sugar and salt. Simmer for 5-7 minutes. Serve hot.

Fish in Green Masala

Serves 4

Ingredients

750g/1lb 10oz swordfish, skinned and filleted

Salt to taste

1 tsp turmeric

50g/1¾oz mint leaves

100g/3½oz coriander leaves

12 garlic cloves

5cm/2in root ginger

2 large onions, sliced

5cm/2in cinnamon

1 tbsp poppy seeds

3 cloves

500ml/16fl oz water

3 tbsp refined vegetable oil

Method

- Marinate the fish with the salt and turmeric for 30 minutes.
- Grind together the remaining ingredients, except the oil, with enough water to form a thick paste.
- Heat the oil in a saucepan. Add the paste and fry on a medium heat for 4-5 minutes. Add the marinated fish and the remaining water. Mix well and simmer for 20 minutes, stirring occasionally. Serve hot.

Clams Masala

Serves 4

Ingredients

500g/1lb 2oz clams, cleaned (see <u>cooking techniques</u>)

Salt to taste

¾ tsp turmeric

1 tbsp coriander seeds

3 cloves

2.5cm/1in cinnamon

4 black peppercorns

2.5cm/1in root ginger

8 garlic cloves

60g/2oz fresh coconut, grated

2 tbsp refined vegetable oil

1 large onion, finely chopped

500ml/16fl oz water

Method

- Steam (see <u>cooking techniques</u>) the clams in a steamer for 20 minutes. Sprinkle salt and turmeric on top of them. Set aside.
- Grind together the remaining ingredients, except the oil, onion and water.
- Heat the oil in a saucepan. Add the ground paste and onion. Fry on a medium heat for 4-5 minutes. Add the steamed clams and fry for 5 minutes. Add the water. Cook for 10 minutes and serve hot.

Fish Tikka

Serves 4

Ingredients

2 tsp ginger paste

2 tsp garlic paste

1 tsp garam masala

1 tsp chilli powder

2 tsp ground cumin

2 tbsp lemon juice

Salt to taste

1kg/2¼lb monkfish, skinned and filleted

Refined vegetable oil for shallow frying

2 eggs, whisked

3 tbsp semolina

Method

- Mix the ginger paste, garlic paste, garam masala, chilli powder, cumin, lemon juice and salt. Marinate the fish with this mixture for 2 hours.
- Heat the oil in a frying pan. Dip the marinated fish in the egg, roll in the semolina and shallow fry on a medium heat for 4-5 minutes.
- Flip and fry for 2-3 minutes. Drain on absorbent paper and serve hot.

Aubergine Stuffed with Prawns

Serves 4

Ingredients

4 tbsp refined vegetable oil

1 large onion, finely grated

2 tsp ginger paste

2 tsp garlic paste

1 tsp turmeric

½ tsp garam masala

Salt to taste

1 tsp tamarind paste

180g/6½oz prawns, shelled and de-veined

60ml/2fl oz water

8 small aubergines

10g/¼oz coriander leaves, chopped, to garnish

Method

- For the stuffing, heat half the oil in a saucepan. Add the onion and fry on a low heat till brown. Add the ginger paste, garlic paste, turmeric and garam masala. Sauté for 2-3 minutes.
- Add the salt, tamarind paste, prawns and water. Mix well and simmer for 15 minutes. Set aside to cool.
- With a knife, make a cross at one end of an aubergine. Cut deeper along the cross, leaving the other end unsevered. Stuff the prawn mixture into this cavity. Repeat for all the aubergines.
- Heat the remaining oil in a frying pan. Add the stuffed aubergines. Fry on a low heat for 12-15 minutes, turning occasionally. Garnish and serve hot.

Prawns with Garlic & Cinnamon

Serves 4

Ingredients

250ml/8fl oz refined vegetable oil

1 tsp turmeric

2 tsp garlic paste

Salt to taste

500g/1lb 2oz prawns, shelled and de-veined

2 tsp ground cinnamon

Method

- Heat the oil in a saucepan. Add the turmeric, garlic paste and salt. Fry on a medium heat for 2 minutes. Add the prawns and cook for 15 minutes.
- Add the cinnamon. Cook for 2 minutes and serve hot.

Sole Steamed in Mustard

Serves 4

Ingredients

1 tsp ginger paste

1 tsp garlic paste

¼ tsp red chilli paste

2 tsp English mustard

2 tsp lemon juice

1 tsp mustard oil

Salt to taste

1kg/2¼lb lemon sole, skinned and filleted

25g/scant 1oz coriander leaves, finely chopped

Method

- Mix together all the ingredients, except the fish and the coriander leaves. Marinate the fish with this mixture for 30 minutes.
- Place the fish in a shallow dish. Steam (see <u>cooking techniques</u>) in a steamer for 15 minutes. Garnish with the coriander leaves and serve hot.

Yellow Fish Curry

Serves 4

Ingredients

100ml/3½fl oz mustard oil

1kg/2¼lb salmon, skinned and filleted

4 tsp English mustard

1 tsp ground coriander

1 tsp chilli powder

2 tsp garlic paste

125g/4½oz tomato purée

120ml/4fl oz water

Salt to taste

1 tsp turmeric

2 tbsp coriander leaves, finely chopped, to garnish

Method

- Heat the oil in a frying pan. Add the fish and fry on a low heat till golden brown. Flip and repeat. Drain the fish and set aside. Reserve the oil.
- Mix the mustard with the ground coriander, chilli powder and garlic.

- Heat the oil used for frying the fish. Fry the mustard mixture for a minute.
- Add the tomato purée. Fry on a medium heat for 4-5 minutes.
- Add the fried fish, water, salt and turmeric. Mix well and simmer for 15-20 minutes, stirring occasionally.
- Garnish with the coriander leaves. Serve hot.

Rassa

(Cauliflower and Peas in Sauce)

Serves 4

Ingredients

2 tbsp refined vegetable oil plus extra for deep frying

250g/9oz cauliflower florets

2 tbsp fresh coconut, grated

1cm/½in root ginger, crushed

4-5 green chillies, slit lengthways

2-3 tomatoes, finely chopped

400g/14oz frozen peas

1 tsp sugar

Salt to taste

Method

- Heat the oil for deep frying in a saucepan. Add the cauliflower. Deep fry on a medium heat till golden brown. Drain and set aside.

- Grind the coconut, ginger, green chillies and tomatoes. Heat 2 tbsp oil in a saucepan. Add this paste and fry for 1-2 minutes.
- Add the cauliflower and the remaining ingredients. Mix well. Cook on a low heat for 4-5 minutes. Serve hot.

Doodhi Manpasand

(Bottle Gourd in Sauce)

Serves 4

Ingredients

3 tbsp refined vegetable oil

3 dried red chillies

1 large onion, finely chopped

500g/1lb 2oz bottle gourd*, chopped

¼ tsp turmeric

2 tsp ground coriander

1 tsp ground cumin

½ tsp chilli powder

½ tsp garam masala

2.5cm/1in root ginger, finely chopped

2 tomatoes, finely chopped

1 green pepper, cored, deseeded and finely chopped

Salt to taste

2 tsp coriander leaves, finely chopped

Method

- Heat the oil in a saucepan. Fry the red chillies and onion for 2 minutes.
- Add the remaining ingredients, except the coriander leaves. Mix well. Cook on a low heat for 5-7 minutes. Garnish with the coriander leaves. Serve hot.